StressFire

by
Massad F. Ayoob

StressFire Photo Credits:
David Price, Dorothy Ayoob, Bert Jenkerson,
Bill Dorvillier

About the Cover: Ayoob, wearing "Wolf's Ears that reduce
gunfire to 85 db yet amplify small sounds, and are ideal for
stalking criminals in the dark, fires one round of Federal 125-
grain, .357 Magnum from 4" barrel S&W model 13 revolver.
Bill Dorvillier took photo hand-held with Canon A1 camera
using Ektachrome 400 film at f./2 on "B". In total darkness,
gun flash provides only illumination for photo.

Available from   **Police Bookshelf**
                 P.O. Box 122
                 Concord, NH 03301 USA

ISBN 0-936279-03-6

To my father, Massad George Ayoob, who taught me the gun, the knife, and the fact that power and responsibility are commensurate.

Foreword

by Ray Chapman, former
World Combat Pistol Champion

I first met Massad Ayoob at a practice session for the 1978 International Practical Shooting Confederation National Championships in Southern California. At that time, he was ranked second in the Northeast section of IPSC. At one point, he was shooting the Unique Mover, an extremely complicated course that involved several targets including two that moved, about fifteen rounds of ammunition, and extremely quick shooting.

I watched him shoot it in 15 seconds with pretty good hits, and knowing that I had recently been World Champion, he then asked me if I saw room for improvement. I gave him a couple of tips involving how to place his feet and how to jump and land in a good firing position after sprinting between two firing points. On his next run, Massad did it in 11 seconds with all center hits.

His ability to instantly absorb and use that information so effectively, impressed me, but so did a few other things. You seldom see a famous "gun writer" shooting in competition like Massad. He had the courage and skill to not only shoot in public, but to do well enough to win a slot in the prestigious Nationals. Also, among a field of shooters with highly sophisticated competition guns and quick draw holsters, he was using the same .45 automatic and service police holster he carried on duty. I later learned that his ability to analyze, refine, develop, and teach shooting techniques was one of his most important talents.

A year later, we met again at the first Bianchi Cup International Pistol Tournament hosted at my Chapman Academy in Columbia, MO. Massad fired the first shot in that historic first Cup, that since has become known as the richest and most prestigious handgun shooting event in the world, and referred to by many as the "Wimbledon of Pistol Shooting." He is the only gun writer who has competed in every Bianchi Cup since, and one of the only three nationally famous instructors (the other two being Mickey Fowler and John Shaw) to have done so. He has always done well there. One year, he was the only shooter using a 4" .357 service revolver in a duty holster, yet finished in the top third of a field made up of the 200 best, and best equipped, combat shooters in the free world. The following year, using borrowed magazines in a pistol that had arrived the day before the Cup started, he was able to shoot down 45 of 48 falling plates, despite no fewer than five jams.

Not long after the second Bianchi Cup, Massad and I shot as partners in the 2-man team events at the Second Chance National Street Combat Shoot in Michigan. We shot three times, placing 5th with our best score and finishing in the prize money with the other two. We worked together so well that I invited him to attend my Advanced Pistol Course in Columbia.

He arrived there with a fresh compound fracture in his right trigger finger, and gamely shot the entire, demanding course weak-handed only with a borrowed revolver he'd never shot before. Yet he finished in the top third of the class against men firing auto-matics free style, and placed second in the gruelling man on man shootoff. Though most of the rest of the class were accomplished combat handgunners, they were shaken by Ayoob's ability to shrug off pain and handicap, and win bout after bout not by speed, but by deadly accurate shot placement under pressure. I had not thought a performance like his would have been possible, and my admira-tion for him grew.

Massad is one of the few who are equally adept with both revolver and autoloading pistol. I have seen him, with a 4" S&W service revolver, win the speed match at the Missouri State Police Practical Shooting Championships, shooting two targets twice each in the chest and once each in the head, one handed in 2¼ seconds for the six shots, including time to react to the start signal and draw from a snapped police holster. I have seen him, with an H&K 9mm. auto, outshoot such great champions as John Shaw on the moving target at Bianchi Cup.

Prior to Massad's coming to the Advanced course, I had read his book, "In the Gravest Extreme," and found it to be the best thing ever written about the use of a gun by a private citizen in self defense. We decided to team up in April of 1981 and conduct a course for responsible citizens who kept guns for personal protec-tion. That first course, which we call the "Armed Citizen" program, was nationally telecast on ABC's "20/20", and was the first of many that we continued to do. It also convinced Massad to open his own school, the Lethal Force Institute, later that year.

Finding that our teaching techniques and credentials strongly complemented one another's, we began teaching a five-day, high-stress Officer Survival Course once a year, and offering two-day seminars in Advanced Officer Survival to police around the country, the latter under the auspices of the Police Marksman Association. Mas is a superb lecturer, and his ability to hold the attention of hardened, cynical officers and tactics instructors while teaching Officer Survival are proven in each class. Many will nod in wide-eyed recognition as he defines some aspect of stress in gunfighting that they have experienced in their own shootouts, but had never fully understood before.

The longer I work with Massad, the more I admire his ability to study, absorb and analyze a shooting technique, to change and adapt and improve one, or to develop a new technique and refine it. I am proud to say that he now teaches several techniques I developed, including the rollover prone, the modified Weaver as an option or complement to his own favorite stances, my methods of shooting on the run and running to a firing point, and my flashlight technique. At the same time, I have adopted some of Massad's methods, as well. These include the use of the Isosceles position as an option to the modified Weaver under stress, the Wedge hold, the StressFire revolver reload, the Ayoob Flashlight Technique, and methods of turning to engage a problem, either to each flank or behind you.

Mas has been a pioneer in exploring physio-psychological responses to danger, and adapting that knowledge to reinforced techniques of the handgun for use under stress. He has also done more than any other expert I'm aware of to integrate traditional martial arts principles with the use of the practical handgun.

In "StressFire," Massad has managed to put into textbook form subjects that are very difficult to teach, many of which have never been in print before, and many of which can only be learned today at the most advanced academies. No matter what else you do, shot placement is the critical thing in what Mas calls stress fire, and this book will help you maintain the mental and physical control to achieve that in a moment of enormous, terrifying pressure.

In "StressFire," Massad assumes that the reader already knows safe gun handling, and how to watch the front sight and control the trigger, so the book is spent in advanced techniques. He also leaves to you, your choice of revolver or auto and what type of holster, and concentrates on how to do well under stress with whatever equipment you have.

Reading and re-reading this book, and carefully practicing what it teaches, will make you a better and more versatile pistol shot. If you carry a gun in a dangerous occupation, it may also save your life one day.

Ray Chapman
Columbia, MO. 1984

Ray Chapman, the first world champion of the combat pistol, has won more than 200 combat matches, and set some 20 national records. He is considered by many the finest pistolcraft instructor in America.

Table of Contents

Chapter 1

Principles of StressFire

At what I now know to have been the tender age of 23, I knew law enforcement was the profession for me. I also knew that I wanted to write, and that I wanted to comfortably support my new wife and our planned family. At about that point, I was given the chance of a lifetime: to go to work for a series of police professional journals doing articles for, and about, cops.

The salary was as much as the police chief I worked for was making at the time. The assignment: to travel the country at the publisher's expense, seeking out the newest and most innovative approaches to police training and procedures. Weaponry, I was told, was to be emphasized: the publisher knew that cops were into gun stuff, and they were especially eager for real-life accounts of gun battles.

Thus began a ten-year period of living a police weapons instructor's dream: travelling around the US and abroad finding out what was really happening, and not having to tell just the police chiefs' side of a bad shooting, whitewashed to cover up policies of poor training and inadequate guns and ammo and holsters.

What I found scared hell out of me.

I found that the conventional American police weapons training worked well on the range, but not worth a damn on the street. I talked to men who had fired at point-blank range from the hip — the way they were taught — and missed. I talked to them after their gunshot wounds had healed. They said, over and over, "I can't

1

understand it — I qualified expert shooting one-handed from the hip at seven yards, but I missed the SOB who shot me at seven feet."

Throughout this time, the concepts of "The New Pistolcraft" as developed by Jeff Cooper were slowly making inroads. I firmly believe that the influence of Cooper's writing in the late 1950's and the 1960's led many police to teach two-hand shooting even at point blank range, and no one will ever know how many lives Cooper thus saved by proxy. By the mid-1970's, some departments were teaching Cooper's whole isometric New Pistolcraft technique.

In 1981, the Federal Bureau of Investigation abandoned the "FBI Method" they had made classic in American Law Enforcement, going almost lock, stock and barrel to the Cooper Methods.

A year before, I had been the sole expert witness testifying on behalf of the plaintiffs in *Christine Hansen et. al.* v. *FBI*, the landmark case in which several female agents fired for failure to qualify were ordered rehired on the basis that the FBI's weapons training was sexist and less than modern. More to the point, the ruling in *Hansen* ordered the FBI to revise and update their firearms training. Bill Rogers, an ex-FBI agent who had become a top competitor in the International Practical Shooting Confederation (IPSC) shooting that Cooper had fostered, convinced the FBI firearms training staff at Quantico that the New Pistolcraft was the way to go.

In so doing, unfortunately, FBI ignored one basic fact: the isometric New Pistolcraft techniques work well only for an extremely well-trained and well-practiced individual. The "Weaver Stance" requires five to seven isometric coordinates to be fulfilled if one is to index on one's target, and if one or two of those coordinates are not achieved, the shooter may well miss under stress.

During this period, I had the pleasure of personally picking the brains of gunfighting legends like Bill Jordan and Colonel Charles Askins, Jr., Bill Allard and Jim Cirillo of the NYPD Stakeout Squad, Jeff Cooper, and others. I studied with such great teachers as Ray Chapman, and the men responsible for training such huge police departments as the London Metropolitan (Bob Wells), NYCPD (Frank McGee and Tom McTernan), and LAPD (Dick Newell).

In consulting with major police departments, I found that while they were fully aware of the New Pistolcraft techniques, they considered them little better than the old FBI method — too complex to be trained to anyone but a constantly-shooting gun buff if the techniques were to be expected to work under the enormous stress of a real-life, lethal-danger shootout.

2

These people had deeply studied the stress that goes on in the human mind and body under such circumstances, and they found that simpler techniques worked better. NYPD had gone from a mediocre batting average in street combat shootings, to a ratio of eleven dead criminals for every murdered cop: they attributed this largely to having switched, in 1970, to the simple "Turret Technique." LAPD, with an even higher officer survival ratio, also uses the turret.

It was with these undeniable facts in mind that when I sought to put together a new form of combat shooting, I based it on the "old" turret position, instead of the "New Pistolcraft." Those who believe that the New Pistolcraft is the "one true religion" fall back on the argument, "That's the technique that wins open competition."

Be that as it may, we are not talking about competition here. We are talking about gunfighting. In the ten years since NYPD adopted the Turret position, McGee and McTernan studied more than 6,000 violent encounters involving their officers, and empirically validated the fact that the turret works under stress. NO OTHER GUNFIGHTING TECHNIQUE HAS EVER BEEN SO THOROUGHLY PROVEN ON THE STREET, WHERE IT COUNTS.

In my own studies, talking with the survivors, I found that we had made great, glaring errors in our approach to combat shooting. We had ignored the vast body of martial arts expertise built through the centuries, techniques long since developed and refined to allow men to maintain their balance and mobility and composure under stress. We had ignored it simply because those martial artists had not happened to have a gun in their hands.

Perhaps the most tragic mistake of all was that in the history of combat handgun training, from the days of the duelists to the FBI System to the New Pistolcraft, the master instructors had built their training systems on techniques that worked on the artificial proving grounds of the training and competition ranges. When the techniques failed on the street, under stress, it was so easy to say, "We know what works for pure shooting. We can teach our student that. If he can't make it work on the street, that's his problem, because we can't graft on a new set of balls and give him courage."

It was a cruel cop-out. The police firearms instructor, or his counterpart in the private academies, cannot shirk his responsibilities so easily. By definition, he is there to teach not merely markmanship, but COMBAT . . . and combat includes training his student to function in that predictable moment when the fight or flight reflex caused by lethal danger is making his hands tremble and his body coil and convulse internally, and his mind go blank.

3

I took it from the opposite end, the end that had to be taken: *starting* with an understanding of what happens to the human body and mind under the awesome pressure of facing death in a second with only the gun in your hand to stop it, and backspacing from *there* to find techniques that worked under stress.

I had several criteria when I set out to put the StressFire system together. It would have to work under great physio-psychological pressure. It would have to be instinctive, something difficult to achieve since there is no human "instinct" to shoot a gun. It would have to be easy to learn, easy to teach, easy to retain for an indefinite period.

During the time frame mentioned above, I began a more than ten year period as a police weapons training instructor. I learned at the outset that techniques would only be grasped if I could immediately make the student see the superiority of the new method, *make him feel it in his own hands*. I knew he wouldn't truly possess it until he felt it there, and this is why so much of what you are about to read will require you at various intervals to set the book down and feel the techniques with your own hands.

You can do most of it without even firing a shot. I teach StressFire and certify people with it on recognized police-type courses in 300 to 500 rounds, sometimes people who never fired a handgun before, and I'm convinced that I could teach it to most people within a hundred shots if I didn't let them take the extra relays of fire to compare the StressFire techniques to the less efficient holds and positions, in live shooting. One veteran police instructor told me before the course that he felt it took 1,000 rounds minimum to be able to shoot effectively in light so dim one couldn't find a sight picture: he was stunned when he found himself doing it with the StressFire technique after 6 shots, and left my course swearing to convert his entire department to it.

Of the many police instructors I train today through the Lethal Force Institute, I find that virtually all are bringing the StressFire principles of shooting, reloading, and coordination with the flash-light back to their in-service officers and recruits. I think that's because the techniques were built from the ground up to be natural, comfortable, trainable and *workable on the street*.

But I can't really be objective about it, can I? That objective judgement can be rendered only by you.

Read StressFire. Try the techniques. Project yourself into the real world instead of the artificiality of the pistol range . . . and determine for yourself what works on the street, where human lives, instead of pistol trophies, are at stake.

Chapter 2

Stress and the Handgun

When a handgun is used "seriously", it is being used under stress. That stress could be "buck fever" as you aim your .44 Magnum at a mule deer, or the tension of knowing that a "10" hit with your next and final shot will win you the State Pistol Championship, but more likely, you have drawn the gun defensively and the stress you experience stems from a real fear for your very life.

You will find yourself going from a condition of relaxed awareness to Condition Orange, a state of significant anxiety, and thence to the near terror of Condition Black, a death duel in progress.

It is useful to understand the "color codes of danger", a concept first developed by US Marines during the Pacific campaign who designated five levels of danger. In the Pacific at that time was a young Marine officer named Jeff Cooper, who went on to found the New Pistolcraft concept. Cooper was to streamline the codes down to four, an improvement for military use but, ironically, not as well suited to police and civilian danger problems as the original military code, in my opinion.

Condition White: No perception of danger. In white, one is unprepared, and attacked in White, one will probably be annihilated.

Condition Yellow: Relaxed Awareness. If asked your location at any time, you could give it; if asked who was behind you, you could answer without looking. You are not actively looking for danger, but know it could come up. You need not be armed to be in Yellow, but if armed, you certainly should be in Yellow. An armed man in

Condition White is a gun waiting to be taken away. As Cooper has correctly observed, a well-adjusted person can spend all his waking hours in Yellow with no ill effects.

Condition Orange: Unspecified Alert. Glass breaks downstairs at 3 AM: it could be an intruder, or just the pussycat knocking over a vase. But there is reason to expect an as yet unknown danger.

In Orange, your sensory antennae are out: you are looking and listening all around you, hard. You're aware of cover that could be taken by you or your opponent, and of the lanes of potential movement. Your gun may or may not be drawn, but should certainly be accessible.

Condition Red: Armed Encounter. You have encountered a dangerous person you have reason to believe has the ability and opportunity to place you in jeopardy. You will take the cover you were scouting when in Orange and will draw your weapon. Depending on the circumstances, a verbal challenge ("Police! Don't move!") may be your option.

Condition Black: Lethal Assault in Progress. One or more people are trying to kill you. Unless they are holding hostages in front of them or you are unarmed, your indicated response will almost always be to fire.

The Cooper system differs in that conditions Red and Black are combined. This makes great sense in the military, where one usually shoots enemy combatants on sight, but is not the ideal mindset for the American policeman or armed citizen, given the fact that at least 13 out of 14 of their encounters are likely not to require firing.

From Condition Orange on up, you will experience "body alarm reaction". The conscious mind has perceived danger, and the primal brain reacts by increasing metabolic rate: the pulse pounds, blood pressure increases precipitously, concentration seems enhanced. Breathing alters, sometimes almost pantingly, resulting occasionally in hyperventilation and accompanying symptoms of dizziness, numbness of extremities, even fainting.

Adrenalin (epinephrine), the most powerful hormone in the body, is instantly released. Blood flow is diverted into the large muscle groups, and into the viscera, because the body knows that its internal 'furnace' is going to have to churn out a large amount of energy soon. This is what causes chalky, pale faces and cold, clammy hands in persons facing danger: the blood has literally been drained from there and into other parts of the body.

As the adrenalin surges, the body becomes much clumsier. Trembling begins, usually in the weak hand first, then almost instantly in the strong hand, and next in the knees. This cannot be eliminated; ask a doctor or a nurse who has seen adrenalin injected into a patient on the operating table, and they'll tell you of feet drumming and hands vibrating.

Strength increases, as does pain tolerance. The body is gearing up for the ultimate effort.

That effort accompanies the highest form of body alarm reaction, which is called "fight or flight reflex," an instinctive mammalian response to deadly danger. The conscious mind has perceived life-threatening danger and the "survival instinct" commands the body to prepare for an enormously taxing effort: to run harder than it has ever run, or to fight harder than it has ever fought. All the effects of body alarm reaction are now greatly magnified.

It is from fight or flight reflex that we get the documented stories of an old lady lifting a pickup truck off her grandson, or of the ordinary man who, attacked by wasps in his basement, cleared a flight of cellar steps in one leap. From this come also the documented cases of seeming immunity to bullets: the Chicago gunman shot 33 times with 9 mm. softpoints before he went down, the outlaw biker who took 13 solid 9 mm. hollowpoint hits from state troopers before he stopped trying to kill them, or the psycho in Bellevue who absorbed 18 .38 slugs before dying.

In the grip of the fight or flight reflex, pain tolerance goes through the roof, and pulse and blood pressure hit levels that, if sustained, could kill even a healthy man — and are often known to do so in combat, even when the dead young soldier had sustained no actual wound. Physical strength hits superhuman levels, and loss of fine motor coordination becomes great.

Tunnel vision and auditory exclusion occur. This means that survival instinct makes you concentrate so much on the danger you will likely be unaware of other bad guys on your flank, or innocents behind the first bad guy. Similarly, you are likely not to hear warning shouts from others.

Knowing that these things are going to happen — great increase in gross physical strength, great deterioration in dexterity — it becomes almost criminally negligent to teach officers and law abiding armed citizens to defend themselves with combat shooting techniques like the FBI Crouch or the isometric Weaver stance that rely heavily on several dexterity-dependent coordinates being accomplished perfectly to index the weapon with the target under stress. (Index is that which lines the gun up with the target; coordinates are the movements that must be executed to achieve index.)

What is necessary are firing techniques that not only don't depend on fine motor coordination, but actually feed off the increase in coarse strength that comes with the fight or flight reflex. The shoving of the arms out to the target and holding tight, as in the Isosceles hold, is a shooting technique that is solidified by greater gross strength and does not suffer appreciably during coordination loss. Similarly, change-of-position techniques that require various steps or pirouetting like a ballerina simply will not work under great stress, but a technique that allows you to turn by lowering your center of gravity and virtually screwing yourself into the ground, will.

The techniques that make up the system I call StressFire have been adapted from street proven techniques of either gunfighting or the martial arts. As an instructor, I've found them extraordinarly simple to teach compared to the other techniques, leaving me much more of my limited time with the student to prepare him or her for the mental conditioning and tactics that are so critical to surviving a firefight.

Simplicity and natural movement are the key to their success, along with the understanding that you cannot afford to contort yourself into bizarre deep crouches or locked leg isometric holds when facing deadly danger. While such techniques work well on the range, you are practicing for a *fight*, and in a fight, the man who sacrifices mobility and balance is likely to lose.

Chapter 3

Techniques for Coping With Stress

In each course I give, there will be some people who are showing definite stress symptoms on the range under the pressure of shooting, before the judgement of their peers. Among these are rapid breathing, licking of the lips, tense facial expressions, sweaty palms, and above all, trembling hands. There will also be pros on the line, experienced combat shooters who handle it so coolly and steadily that they're almost arrogant.

"Don't be ashamed that your hands are trembling and it's obvious that you're nervous," I'll tell the class. "Pity the honcho who *doesn't* feel scared and show it. You see, those of you whose hands are shaking will leave here knowing that even if your fingers are trembling with fear, you can still control the gun well enough to drive your bullets into the center of a man-size target — and the pistol whiz who feels in control here will never know if he can do that until his life is on the line in a dark alley — and that's a hell of a time to find out!"

The best piece of advice that I can give my students never fails to shock them. "If you're serious about learning to shoot under pressure," I tell them, "never *practice* with a pistol again!"

The rationale for that statement is based on coping with stress. Mere "practice" with a gun is just ballistic masturbation: you're going through the movements, but you're not accomplishing

9

anything or learning anything useful to remember and apply later when it counts. A character in the play, "The Boys in the Band", makes the statement, "The nice thing about masturbation is that you don't have to look your best." That's just what's wrong with pistol practice: nothing is on the line when you fire, and there's no compelling motivation to do your best.

Let me give you "Ayoob's Law" about learning to shoot under stress: "EVERYTIME YOU FIRE A SHOT, SOMETHING SHOULD RIDE ON IT!" Shooting in matches may not be your cup of tea, but the tremors induced by an audience and a rich prize pot will throw you into a pressure cooker that will temper you and your nerves like steel in a crucible, and make you hard.

If your preparation for the match is mere "practice", then when you get to the actual firing line, you'll be thinking, consciously or subconsciously, "This is *it*! This is the moment of truth! This is what all that practice was leading up to! The *big moment*, do or die . . ." That sort of mindset will destroy you under pressure.

Suppose, instead, that you have to shoot every weekend in a match . . . or, if that isn't possible, make every practice session a stress-test. You can do that by shooting against a friend for bets: boxes of primers, a dollar a stage, a six-pack, anything. If you have a shoot alone, do what I do: save your targets, and pay your wife a dollar for every shot outside the ten ring (or, if that's not in the cards, earmark a buck per point or a quarter per point lost, for charity).

This will soon condition you to the basic truth of stress shooting: every shot counts, every shot must be delivered, every shot that flies past the center mark will cost you something.

It doesn't take too much of this to get you tempered. Soon, shooting under pressure is no longer the "big moment that everything else in life led up to" like a terrifying crescendo of emotion. Now, *pressure has become the norm*. You will one day find yourself on the line at a match, and instead of thinking, "Oh, my God, this is *it*," you'll think, "Geez, here I am at another pistol match . . . I wonder why all these other guys on the firing line look so nervous?"

At that moment, you will have arrived; you will have mastered stress by embracing it and making it a part of your life, a part you control and channel.

Some degree of stress will always be there; Masters don't fear it, they welcome it. Asked when he first lost his "match nerves", world champion Ray Chapman replied, "Never, and I hope I never do. I welcome those little tremors in my hand as I go to the line in a 'moment of truth' match. It means the adrenalin is surging that will make me stronger and faster, and 'stronger and faster' are two components of 'championship form'. I know that if I just hold the gun firmly, with the greater strength that comes from the adrenalin surge, and focus on my front sight, any trembling in my hands is just going to tremble those bullets right into the X-ring."

How does this relate to shooting for your life on the street? Quite simply, it means that as you go into the danger scene, you can think to yourself confidently, "My hand may be shaking, but I know from experience that if my hands are trembling under pressure, I can still put the bullets where they have to go!" That confidence leaves your mind free to deal with tactical matters of movement, cover, and outflanking and surprising the enemy, making you a much more flexible and effective fighter. Confidence born of controlled experience is one of the keys to survival of a violent encounter.

There are also some physical tricks to further reducing tension. One of them, which some practice ritually before the match, is what martial artists call "ki breathing". One such technique is to tense all your muscles rigidly, take a deep breath, and hold it for as long as you can. This helps develop steely, tremor-free nerves, and reduce panting when afflicted by body alarm reactions.

Another useful technique is an exercise that comes from "sanchin", the internal strengthening discipline of karate. Take a deep breath, place your palms together in front of your chest, and press them together as hard as you can with dynamic tension for as long as you can hold your breath.

A trick you can use more often under more circumstances is to clench your fists as tight as you can, with a sympathetic tightening of muscles all the way up the arms. Curl the fists inward for maximum muscle tension. Hold as hard as you can for as long as you can; then, "shake out" your hands and arms as you would in a gymnasium warmup exercise. This is an effective physical stress outlet, and loosens up muscles and tendons, making them quicker to reach in the next few moments when you have to go for your gun.

When the moment comes to prepare to draw, *don't* lock your hands into a gunfighter's claw. This will exaggerate trembling, since flexor muscles are stronger than the extensor muscles you're using to hold the fingers open. Besides, you'll have to unlock that claw before you can start the scoop of the holstered weapon.

A boxer doesn't stand ready with his fists tightly clenched: his fingers are loose, and will only tighten as the punch is launched. This gives him added flexibility for speed and accuracy of the blow, and the tightening of the hand adds power to his strike. Apply this to the pistol: let the fingers hang relaxed at the end of your hand. You may look like the limp-wristed pistol champion of

Fire Island, but the tremors will disappear completely, and your movement to the gun will be much more smooth, fluid and positive. The almost insolent appearance of total relaxation seems to have a rather unnerving effect on one's opponents, as well.

There's one more breathing technique that will be useful for your stress repertoire. Under stress, many people breathe too rapidly, causing hyperventilation with the symptoms of dizziness, numb fingers, loss of coordination, and even panic. A doctor would tell you to breathe into a paper bag, but that's going to look almost as silly on a pistol range as in a dark alley.

The martial artist's equivalant of breathing into a paper bag to fight hyperventilation by restoring oxygen/CO_2 balance, is this: take a breath, then slowly and fiercely "hiss it out". Apart from its physiological effect, it looks to the opposition like the Attack of the Cat People.

"Shitfire, Billy Bob, let's leave this dude alone. The mutha's either *crazy*, or he's gonna have a *seizure*!" Be sure and warn your patrol partners and teammates beforehand that you may be using this technique . . .

Chapter 4

Body Positioning

Because the hands and body will tremble under stress, perhaps violently, and lose coordination, it is obvious that two-hand holds should be employed wherever possible. Numerous techniques have been tried.

There are three two-handed techniques currently in use: the Weaver Stance; the modified Weaver as exemplified at its best by the Chapman Position; and the Isosceles hold, best applied with a total-body Turret Stance.

WEAVER STANCE

First developed by LA Sheriff's Deputy Jack Weaver during the late 1950's, and refined and promulgated by Col. Jeff Cooper, the Weaver Stance was the first of the deliberately isometric modern techniques. As taught by Cooper, it has seven to eight coordinates:

1. feet are in a boxer's stance vis-a-vis the target;
2. legs are locked, at the knees;
3. firing arm is slightly bent;
4. support arm is sharply bent;
5. elbow of support arm is tucked into body, perpendicular to ground;
6. strong hand pushes out, with 40-45 lb. of pressure;
7. weak hand pulls in, with 40-45 lb. of pressure; and
8. since bent arms may lower position of gun, head may have to be tilted to the side, a move which allows a faster sight pickup in any case.

The good news with the Weaver is that the bent arms and the isometric tension of the pushing and pulling muscles

13

Hold 1: Cooper version of Weaver hold. Author feels unlocked, extended thumbs reduce control of weapon.

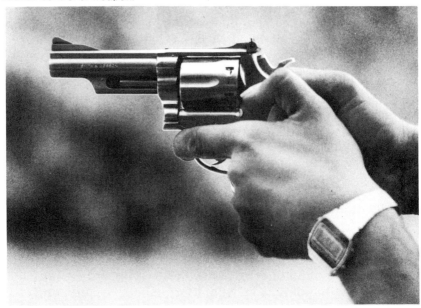

Hold 2: Chapman hold. Thumbs are locked down (much better) and index finger is in front of trigger guard to help hold muzzle down. However, this finger placement works poorly with revolvers due to rounded trigger guard, and also does not adapt to locked-arms Isosceles position. Chapman Academy now teaches Ayoob Wedge for revolver shooters.

14

Hold 3: Kevin Murphy of Super Vel demonstrates the thumb cross over hold.

Hold 4: In most cases, best place for support hand thumb is curled down over firing thumb, says author. This is extremely fast, and increases strength of support hand fingers, since thumb is not hyperextended. Thumb crossover grip, shown, is recommended by author only for very small revolvers or very hard-kicking guns.

Hold 5: Bent arms of Weaver Stance, seen from below: shock absorber effect reduces recoil; however, latitude for turning to engage multiple assailants is greatly diminished.

Hold 6: Isosceles hold, so called because locked arms form an isosceles triangle with the chest.

16

Hold 7: The Weaver Stance. Feet are in boxer's position, weak side sharply forward; strong elbow slightly bent; weak elbow sharply bent; weak arm perpendicular to ground; strong hand pushes out, and weak hand pulls back, w/ 40-45 lb. pressure; head may be tilted slightly for faster sight acquisition. Author feels that is all too many coordinates to work well under extreme stress.

Hold 8: Chapman Position is an improved Weaver. Edgeways stance to target is not so pronounced. Firing arm is locked; support arm pulls into shoulder as if firing arm was rifle stock. Foot position, lock, pull; only 3 coordinates, a decided improvement over the classic Weaver's 6.

17

Hold 9: In the Turret stance, using Isosceles hold, there is only one coordinate: shove the gun out in front of you until it stops. Foot position takes care of itself, with the legs balancing the body as the torso turns like a turret on the gun mount of the pelvis. Ideally, says Ayoob, it should be used as shown, in the Advancing Assault position. Upper body is isosceles turret, feet are placed as if firing a shotgun.

18

Hold 10: Combat shotgun stance: body leans forward, rear leg is straight, lead leg is bent forward. This absorbs recoil shock for quicker recovery, and "coils" the body for instant, dynamic movement in any direction under fire.

create a shock absorber effect that significantly reduces felt recoil and snaps the firing gun quickly back on target. Since the gun is closer to the body, it feels lighter and in fact exerts less leverage weight on bent arms than it would on fully extended limbs.

The bad news? The Weaver, for several reasons, tends to fall apart under extreme stress. With those conditions prevailing, the essential boxer's stance cannot always be achieved. Without moving the feet, one finds the ability to traverse is extremely limited — to 90 degrees or even less for some people.

Under stress, with exaggerated gross strength movements and loss of coordination, the strong arm tends to overpower the weak arm, sending the Weaver shooter's bullets high left if he's right handed. The exaggerated push-pull of the technique also increases muscle tremor. Raising of the weak elbow allows greater traverse but unlocks the hold, reducing accuracy for most people. Finally, the sharply edgeways stance exposes an armored-officer's unprotected whole or upper side to the opposing gunfire.

CHAPMAN METHOD

The most sensible of the many variations of "modified Weaver" hold, the Chapman has only three coordinates that need to be remembered:
1. slight boxer's stance;
2. firing arm is rigidly locked; and
3. weak hand pulls firing arm into shoulder, like a rifle stock.

Tremors are greatly reduced in this position, which is also simpler, quicker, and more natural to get into than the classic Weaver. It also allows a 180° traverse, and permits the head to be held up, a more natural and instinctive position. It does not open the unprotected or semi-protected side of an armored man to opposing gunfire nearly so much as the Weaver.

ISOSCELES

There is only one coordinate for the Isosceles hold: thrust both arms straight in front of you until they can go no farther. The hands are now equidistant from the body, and neither can overpower the other. It is the one technique that will not be broken by stress, when the surge of body strength exaggerates the thrust of the gun to the target. Loss of coordination is irrelevant since there are no complex positions to hold, and the greater strength is no longer something to fight, but now something to harness: it simply holds the gun tighter and steadier on target.

Proponents of the Weaver have given the Isosceles a bad name by demonstrating it the wrong way: with the shoulders

Turret 1: Ayoob shows how with turret stance developed by Fairbairn and popularized in US by McGee, a man facing 12 o'clock can instantly swivel and take out antagonist at 4 o'clock w/ Isosceles hold. Note that knees have flexed and pelvis has dropped instinctively to maintain balance.

Turret 2: Notice that turret stance and Isosceles hold guarantee full torso coverage against enemy's fire when Second Chance vest is worn. Author finds Isosceles Turret most adaptable for the armored gunfighter, Chapman modified Weaver a close second and the classic Weaver stance a poor and distant third.

StressFire Turret 1: Use of Turret allows best latitude for return fire when searching stairwell. Ayoob begins w/proper "movement mode": back to wall, moving up sideways, feet two steps apart.

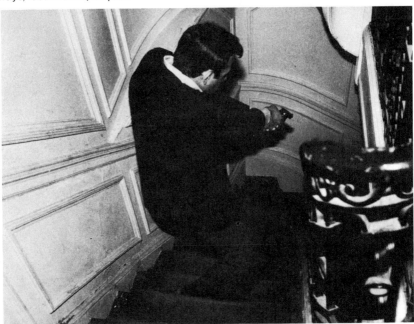

StressFire Turret 2: From here, simple turreting at the hips allows him to instantly respond to attack from below . . .

StressFire Turret 3: ... or from above. Note that no repositioning of feet is necessary; lower body instinctively maintains balance.

cantilevered backward to balance the weight of the gun, a method often seen used by PPC shooters, who fire very heavy revolvers with very light loads. That position allows a *combat* gun to literally kick one backward when fired with hot loads.

For stress combat shooting, the Isosceles should be applied in a slight crouch, with the legs unlocked. Indeed, under stress, it *will* be! At the first hint of danger, it is human nature to crouch forward to a greater or lesser degree; this is nature's way of minimizing your exposure to injury, and balancing you to fight or to flee.

You have never seen a runner run, or a boxer fight, with their torso bolt upright and their legs locked, yet this is the way Weaver aficionadoes expect you to shoot. Is it any wonder that the Weaver technique tends to come apart when the shooter experiences body alarm reaction to a stress situation?

With the torso bent at the waist and the gun straight out ahead in both hands, the body is balanced by the flexed knees, which automatically compensate for balance by lowering the center of body gravity, in the pelvis. The technique can be made even stronger by taking a step toward the target with the weak leg and, bending it sharply, applying weight forward.

The body is now poised to move instantly forward, back, or from side to side, and a considerable portion of upper body weight, coupled with the muscular tension of the locked arms, snaps even a hard kicking pistol back on target at least as quickly as does the Weaver stance, with its practitioner standing erect.

The total position is known as the "turret," popularized in this country by Frank McGee, the legendary master firearms instructor of NYPD. The theory is that it allows the widest traverse when the shooter must swing his gun between multiple opponents; the foot position is essentially irrelevant, since the body pivoting on the torso has become a "tank turret" that pivots on the "gun mount" of the pelvic axis. The feet are merely the treads that bring the tank to the scene of firing; as the body turns, the knees will automatically flex to instantly maintain body balance without having to think about it.

In StressFire, that forward step is called the Advancing Assault position. It would be made if you had time to anticipate the danger, and were in an agressor's position to initiate a challenge, standing in a "police interrogation position," or were about to fire on a shooting range. Essentially, the body is in an Isosceles from the waist up, and a combat shotgun position from the waist down.

MAKING A CHOICE

While some people will fire better with one technique on the range, and some with another, we are finding that the straight-arms Isosceles position seems to work best under extreme stress. The great, contemporary gunfighting authority John Farnam, himself a devotee of the Weaver stance, has admitted in print that the Isosceles holds up better under extreme pressure. So does Chapman, developer of the best technique in the Weaver family, who calls the Isosceles "the stress position."

However, as the reader will shortly see, having a full repertoire of fighting techniques for use under stress is superior to using one technique only. A comprehensive knowledge of the Weaver, and the Chapman, *and* the Isosceles — as taught at LFI — allows one to move smoothly and fluidly between the techniques without effort or even conscious thought, the way a trained boxer instantly follows a left jab with a well executed right cross. For instance, a man levelled on a target at 12 o'clock with an Isosceles can pivot at the waist without moving his feet and aim at a man behind him at six o'clock, *if* he can flow smoothly into a reverse-stance Weaver (see Pivot Strikes).

In StressFire training, we have found the strongest use of the Weaver to be in traversing techniques, where the torso has been twisted and the arms have been turned into a maximum torque position to meet an attack from the flank. With the body so torqued, one no longer has to make a conscious effort to maintain equal pressure between the hands, and fight the body's natural tendency for the strong hand to overpower the weak hand; *the body creates its own dynmanic tension, making the Weaver, at last, stress-proof*! This will be proven the first time you try the StressFire Star technique, shown elsewhere in these pages.

One-handed and position shooting will be discussed elsewhere in this book. We suggest, however, that the reader be familiar with the Isosceles, *and* the Weaver, *and* the Chapman method; else, he will never be a consummately skilled combat shooter. A shooter who can fire from only Weaver or only Isosceles is like a boxer whose only good punch is a jab *or* a hook.

FLEXED KNEES

For decades, police firearms instructors taught a deep crouch that resembled someone defecating in the woods. They justified it on the grounds that (a) since they were teaching hip shooting, anything less than a deep crouch failed to extend the arm toward an opponent's body; (b) it made a smaller target; and (c) if the officer was shot, he would fall forward instead of backward.

We now know all three premises to be false. Hip shooting isn't quicker than eye-level shooting in the practical sense, so needn't be provided for at all; bending forward to make a smaller target increases the time that you're going to *be* a target before you shoot and neutralize the danger, and in any case means that a bullet striking you will traverse downward through your torso, striking more organs and significantly increasing the chance of your death; finally, if you are hit, you can return fire a lot more easily if you fall on your back than if you fall on your face.

A man who has fallen prone must raise his whole pain-racked upper body and tilt his head awkwardly back; the wounded combatant who has fallen supine needs only cast his eyes downward, raise his pistol a few degrees, and shoot his tormentor.

It turns out, however, that FBI was teaching the right thing, even if for the wrong reasons. *The crouch makes sense because the human body in the grip of body alarm reaction will crouch anyway, and the shooter should be trained to fire from that position!* Major W. E. Fairbairn first observed this phenomenon when one of his raid teams revisited an alley in Shanghai which they had moved cautiously down the night before. Fairbairn discovered a set of clotheslines that would have strangled a standing man ... but his raiders, in the grip of body alarm reaction, had instinctively been crouching so sharply that all passed completely under it!

It is difficult to reconcile teaching a combat shooter to fire standing on locked legs, in light of what we know about human physiology and the fight or flight reflex. Locked legs are fulcrums of leverage that hamper the ability to move instantly. One of my assistant instructors, Jerry Chinn of the Southwest Pistol League, is also a Tai Chi Chuan practitioner.

Jerry puts our LFI students through a balance exercise, man on man. One student takes a firing position, while the other grasps his arms and attempts to move him about. The object is for the first not to fight, but to maintain balance and keep his empty hands "aimed" at his opponent's center chest. With the legs locked in a Classic Weaver, the first student will be toppled sideways like a helpless robot; yet, as soon as he unlocks his legs, he can easily maintain balance completely and effortlessly.

Notice that the deep crouch of the old FBI training is not at all necessary; merely unlocking the knees suffices. As the body needs balance, the legs will find it, either bending the knees more deeply or turning the feet slide sideways. ALWAYS REMEMBER THAT, IN A FIGHT, BALANCE AND MOBILITY MUST NEVER BE SACRIFICED.

HAND HOLDS

One book published as recently as 1981 on combat shooting suggested that the support hand grasp the wrist of the strong

T'ai Chi 1: Author shows T'ai Chi Chuan exercise to prove need to flex knees. Opponent takes a 2-hand hold and locks knees . . .

T'ai Chi 2: . . . and opponent is easily levered off balance, since his locked knees have made fulcrums of his legs.

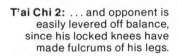

T'ai Chi 3: Try same exercise with the "shooter's" legs *unlocked* at the knees, however ...

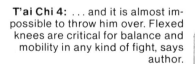

T'ai Chi 4: ... and it is almost impossible to throw him over. Flexed knees are critical for balance and mobility in any kind of fight, says author.

28

hand when firing; gun magazines still show "experts" improperly holding handguns with their palm beneath the butt of the gun. This "cup and saucer" hold lifts the cup from the saucer upon recoil, and offers very little stabilization against the pressure of the trigger pull.

The Weaver hold, in which the knuckles of the support hand are in line with the trigger guard of the pistol, is better, but still has flaws: because the trigger guard is now essentially in the bottom of a dish formed by the index finger and the web of the hand, the gun has excellent vertical stability but not great lateral stability. One often sees Weaver shooters firing groups with excellent vertical control but some horizontal dispersal.

Another problem with the Weaver as commonly taught is keeping the thumbs high, riding the safety of a Colt .45 auto. It is not necessary to ride the safety to keep it down, and the short-comings of this high thumb position are many. First, with the thumb unlocked, the rest of the hand can't maintain the firmest possible hold on the grip. Second, the high thumb pulls the web of the hand away from the grip safety, causing failures to fire. Third, the high thumb tends to ride against the slide, creating friction that can jam the mechanism of the autoloading pistol.

The thumb of the firing hand should be locked down for maximum control of trigger squeeze, aim, and recoil. Similarly, the thumb of the support hand should also be curled down, ideally with its pad resting atop the nail of the strong thumb. This allows the support hand to squeeze more firmly and contribute better to the control of the handgun in every respect.

Try this simple exercise to prove the above statement. Extend your weak hand, and *with the thumb extended*, squeeze the four fingers as tight as you can. Maintain that pressure, and mentally measure it; now, complete the first by slowly locking down your thumb. Feel the pressure increase? That's because the human hand was "built" to work off the opposing thumb, and that's why a position with the thumbs up higher or with the weak thumb extended across the back of the firing hand can weaken your hold, as can strong thumb riding high on the safety.

Besides that, the thumb crossed over the back of the firing hand has a tendency to shift during recoil or under stress, blocking the slide of an auto or the hammer of a double action revolver. Either way, you're asking for a minor injury at best, and at worst, a gun stoppage that can cause your death in a shootout.

The most natural way to grab the gun is a hold I call the Interlocking Wraparound. That is, the support hand wraps around the weak hand, with its fingers interlocking in the groove between the strong hand's fingers. This is natural and instinctive, like

Ayoob Wedge 1: Beginning of Ayoob Wedge hold. Top of middle finger contacts bottom of trigger guard as 3 support fingers take interlocking wraparound hold on firing hand. Index finger comes in from front . . .

Ayoob Wedge 2: . . . and jams itself under trigger guard. This cams the muzzle upward. Don't lower other fingers to make room for index; let index finger make its own room.

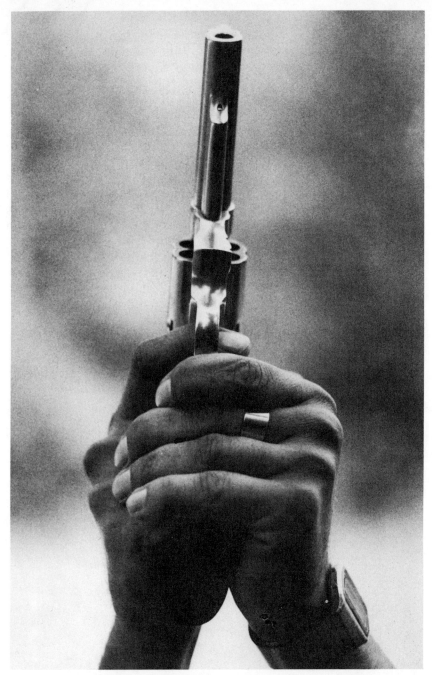

Ayoob Wedge 3: Wedge seen from below. V-shaped wedge of flesh and bone holds gun on target against trigger jerks that would otherwise snap muzzle down or sideways. If you miss the wedge working at speed, you're still in a solid interlocking wraparound hold. Failsafe!

making a two-hand fist.

The one improvement that can be made on it is the Ayoob Wedge. As the illustrations show, this involves grasping in a conventional interlocking wraparound except that the index finger of the support hand is extended. The contact point is upper edge of middle finger against bottom of trigger guard. Now, the extended finger is pulled in tightly beneath the trigger guard. Don't lower the other three support fingers to make room for it; instead, make the finger create its own room. This cams the muzzle upward.

That index finger is now a solid wedge of flesh and bone beneath the trigger guard, holding the entire weapon on target against trigger jerking. It is a very quick fix for someone who has trouble with double-action revolver shooting, and holds any gun steadier. It also reduces the sensation of felt recoil.

The weak thumb would be crossed over the back of the firing hand only if the hands were very large and the gun very small (for comfort), or if the recoil were so violent (as in the case of a .44 Magnum) that the hands threatened to separate if the thumb were not hooking them together.

Practice with these basic holds and stances. Without them, you'll not be able to maximally control a powerful handgun in rapid combat fire. Once you have them, you're ready to proceed into subtleties of firing a handgun under stress.

Chapter 5

Proper Hold When Approaching Danger

Because so much of firearms training for combat has been developed on the range against paper targets instead of with research using real and hostile humans, few people have any real understanding of how to hold someone at gunpoint, or how to "stalk" a suspect in a situation that may soon explode into an armed confrontation.

Many academies teach the student to walk with the gun extended in a two-hand firing position, but with the muzzle down at a 45° angle, when in a "stalking mode." The technique is called "low point." The problem is that most gun battles occur suddenly and at very close range, from contact distance to, typically, 10 feet. That's close enough for an opponent to take you by surprise and grab your gun . . . and when that happens, you *don't* want the weapon locked out in front of you. It doesn't matter if the muzzle is straight out or pointing down; the problem is that your arms are hyperextended, and if the attacker grabs your weapon, all he has to do is jerk his arm back to pull you helplessly off balance. If your muzzle is down, his greater leverage on your gun will prevent you from raising the barrel to bear on him.

The same problem exists with the military-style "Fairbairn/ Applegate" technique. Promulgated most effectively in Rex Applegate's classic book "Kill or Be Killed," this method of holding the gun at the end of a locked arm and bringing it up when you make visual contact with the enemy may work at battlefield distances, but not in close, where the bad guy may get the first move and may

Applegate Stance 1: In Applegate Stance, the best battlefield technique ever developed for one-hand shooting of military pistol, gun arm is locked down . . .

Applegate Stance 2: . . . and then raised to fire when danger threatens. Ayoob found that streets unlike battlefields were too close-quartered for this method to work all the time.

start from a position almost on top of you. Here again, he can nullify your gun and even take it from you rather easily.

That's why, in StressFire, the proper method for holding the gun in "stalking mode" is with the elbow(s) bent. *One handed,* you want the pistol tucked into your hip; an old and valid policemen's trick. Placing the base of your gunhand thumb on the top edge of your belt is a good "felt index" to keep the gun pointed at belly level on a potential attacker. The gun is also close in to your body, very hard for a gun-grabber to get at, and by simply taking a step back with your gun-side leg and straight-arming the attacker in the face with the palm of the other hand, you can get clear of the assault and back into a controlling position.

If the gun is in a two-hand hold, you want it close to your midsection, muzzle up; the "high point" position. To fire, simply thrust the gun out into a turret position, locking both arms: it's lightning fast, and because it stops by itself as the gun hands "reach the end of their string," you don't have the bobbing movement and need to readjust aim that comes when you bring the gun *up* and have to stop it suddenly.

This technique also gives you much greater leverage for fighting off someone who jumps you. You can simply rip the gun back and down, out of the grabbing hand simultaneously raising your elbow in a "can-opener" movement. If necessary, you can use your weak hand to lock the grabber's wrist, which makes it much easier to get your weapon back out of his hand. If the suspect has placed you in deadly danger with a weapon in his other hand, your bent elbows allow you to simply thrust the gun straight forward *through* his grabbing hand, and shoot him in the head.

The principle works the same when using a long gun. If you turn the corner with the rifle or shotgun at the shoulder but with muzzle down, as is recommended by many combat weapons instructors, an opponent who jumps from around the corner and grabs the muzzle has the leverage to jerk you forward off your feet and disarm you. But, with the elbows bent and the gun close to you in a "port arms" position, you can buttstroke him in the groin, shove the muzzle forward into his face, or take advantage of your greater leverage on the shotgun or carbine to execute other weapon retention techniques.

Holding the gun in the StressFire way also greatly reduces the tendency to "lead with your gun," that is, to let the gun muzzle peek around the corner before you do, giving your position away to an observant enemy who can then level his own gun and be ready to blow your head off when you lean out to scan the area. It also eliminates the danger of snagging furniture, etc. with a gun muzzle at low point that you literally can't keep an eye on.

Handgun Low Ready 1: With handgun in low ready position coming around corner...

Handgun Low Ready 2: ... the guy who is faster than you can take you. He has total leverage at the end of your hyperextended arm(s).

Handgun High Ready 1: Author prefers "high ready" position with handgun when stalking in danger situation for several reasons.

Handgun High Ready 2: When attacker around corner grabs gun in high ready position . . .

Handgun High Ready 3: ... author can easily rip gun out of hand using "can opener" or "Lindell #2" defensive weapon retention technique.

Handgun High Ready 4: Alternatively, if gun grabber has his own weapon like this claw hammer, Ayoob trained shooter simply extends his arm forward and thrusts through attacker's hold shooting him in the brain.

Shotgun Low Carry 1: With the shot-gun in low carry . . .

Shotgun Low Carry 2: . . . opponent lurking behind corner controls the gun and can even pull you off balance forward and kill you with contact weapon.

Shotgun High Carry 1: With high shotgun carry in stalking mode . . .

Shotgun High Carry 2: . . . a suspect who grabs shotgun gives you leverage to fight . . .

Shotgun High Carry 3: ... either ripping free with buttstroke to groin (shown) or head ...

Shotgun High Carry 4: ... or if he has a deadly weapon in his other hand ...

Shotgun High Carry 5: ... simply lifting rear end of shotgun and pulling trigger decapitating attacker.

Your hand position on the weapon is also critical to keeping proper control of the scene. You drew the gun because you perceived yourself to be in danger, and that means body alarm reaction or even flight or flight reflex have kicked into gear: you're stronger and faster and meaner, but you're also clumsy and jumpy as hell. A tense person who is startled or thrown off balance tends to respond with convulsive muscular movements, and this could make your gun go off. At best, this is embarassing and can give your position away; at worst, you can shoot an innocent person accidentally. Therefore, *your finger should be off the trigger* when you've drawn your gun to stalk or await a potentially lethal antagonist.

That, by itself, won't guarantee safety against an accidental discharge. I worked as a consultant for the legal defense team of a police sergeant who was charged with improper use of force because, as he approached a potentially dangerous suspect with his Colt .45 service automatic drawn, the man grabbed his weapon. As the sergeant felt the gun being pulled away from him, he instinctively tightened his fist.

The thumb safety had been locked, and his finger was off the trigger and extended. But, as he made that instinctive and defensive "clutch" to keep from losing his weapon, the tightening thumb came down and wiped the safety off into the "fire" position at the same moment that his index finger snapped into the trigger guard. BANG! A 200-grain Speer hollowpoint bullet struck the suspect in the chin, literally tearing off his lower jaw.

The court ruled that the officer had acted properly, in part because the defense presentation made it clear that this could happen to anyone! So much for a mechanical safety preventing accidental discharges.

The problem was that the officer held his finger off the trigger *with the finger straight alongside* the frame, the way taught in most academies. I found four bad points with this technique. First, the extended finger can snag on the trigger guard when coming in to the trigger if it *does* become necessary to fire, and this can slow your response just enough to cost you your life at the hands of a suddenly emerging, armed opponent. Secondly, when you bring the finger to the trigger from this position, in a state of great stress, *the fingertip is moving backward and impacts on the trigger*. This can cause an unintentional discharge of the weapon.

Third, the extended finger can press too hard on the slide stop stud of some auto pistols, loosening the part and causing the pistol to jam or disassemble when the first shot is fired. Fourth, the extended finger in this position will be bent backward and probably broken if someone grabs the gun and twists it, leaving you unable

Finger Off 1: Holding finger on trigger going into stalking situation can be invitation to disaster.

Finger Off 2 & 3: We have always been taught to hold our fingers straight out from the trigger guards, like this. Ayoob found multiple problems with the technique.

44

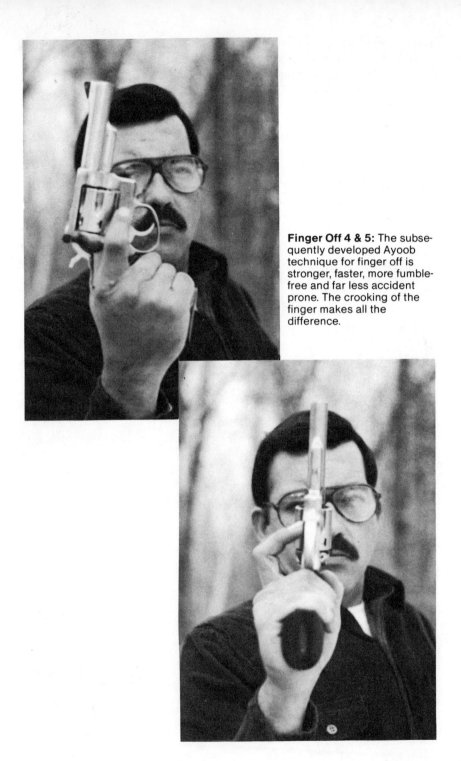

Finger Off 4 & 5: The subsequently developed Ayoob technique for finger off is stronger, faster, more fumble-free and far less accident prone. The crooking of the finger makes all the difference.

to hold on long enough to execute a weapon retention technique.

For the StressFire system, I developed a "trigger finger-off" hold that eliminates all problems. *The trigger finger is out of the triggerguard, and BENT, with the tip of the finger touching the frame just under the cylinder (on revolvers) or just behind the latch or button of the slide stop (on autoloaders).*

Because the bent finger's tip is located directly above the trigger, it doesn't snag on the trigger guard when you do have to go for a fast shot, as happens when the finger is extended forward. Also, because the finger is coming in from the side instead of from the front, it *slides across* the trigger instead of slamming into it. This goes far toward preventing premature discharges. In class demonstrations at Lethal Force Institute, most students find that they can go from that StressFire position to an immediate shot almost as fast as they can fire starting with their finger on the trigger, and much faster than with the finger off the trigger and extended.

With this technique, pressure on the slide stop stud is eliminated. Also, the bent index finger can withstand great pain and torque without sympathetic opening of the hand, helping you to hang onto the gun in a grappling situation.

In 13 out of 14 armed encounters, among civilians, it does not become imperative that the defender fire his gun. Among police, the ratio of gunpoint situations to "shoot" situations is even greater. And for every time you place a man at gunpoint, there will be more times when you stalk a potential suspect with your gun drawn, but do not encounter him.

The above techniques of the StressFire system, designed for use against men instead of targets, in the hands of tense combatants instead of cool-headed target shooters, will go far toward helping you keep from accidentally shooting someone, and toward preventing a violent suspect from taking you off guard and snatching your weapon away to use against you.

Chapter 6

Drawing and Reholstering

Veteran street cops have a saying that the fastest draw is to have the gun already in your hand. That's undeniable, but not having seen the danger in time isn't a mistake you should have to die for. Practice in drawing your weapon under stress is mandatory if you are to protect yourself with it under a variety of circumstances.

There are problems with teaching the draw in stages of "one, two, three" as the hand comes down on the weapon. Better is a smooth, fluid draw with maximum use made of momentum. If you're wearing a hip holster, the hand should describe a circle as it starts from the front of the body, swoops down below and behind the holster, "scoops" the gun, and continues its line of movement up and forward as the gun goes straight to the target.

The "scoop" should not be misunderstood. One does not just hook the gun and try to grasp it in mid-air. Rather, the hand takes a firm hold in proper firing position in every respect *except the finger's off the trigger* before the gun clears leather. In the beginning stages, your hand will come to a dead stop as you take your hold on the gun; in time, you'll feel it become one swift, fluid movement.

TECHNIQUES ACCORDING TO HOLSTER

The technique for clearing the handgun is predicated on where on the anatomy it is carried.

Strong Side, on or behind hip. The most natural and concealable place for most males to carry a sidearm. The hand comes down with the knife-edge of the heel of the palm (so as to slide through the opening of a jacket; much of the time, you'll have a coat on, and you shouldn't practice two draws for different types of clothing).

As the hand scoops the gun in a proper hold, the index finger still extended forward, the muzzle is at about a 45° angle to the ground as the hand goes past the torso. The gun hand continues its forward thrust, and is met by the support hand, which comes in from the *side*, not from the front of the gun. At any point after the 45° angle has been reached, the index finger of the firing hand may slide onto the trigger.

Advantages of this type of draw are: Line of movement is straight and direct toward the target, and carry is very comfortable to most people. Allows gun to be worn discreetly concealed beneath unbuttoned coat.

Strong side, in front of hip. While the butt is usually tilted forward for concealment and comfort when carried behind the hip, it is worn straight up or tilted backward when worn ahead of the hip. This carry, used widely on the American frontier and resurrected for modern competition by Ken Hackathorn, allows the hand to come down and draw the gun with the wrist locked throughout, making for a very positive drawing motion. Favored by such masters of speed draw as Tom Campbell, Mike Plaxco, Ray Chapman, and others, it has the unnerving disadvantage of pointing the gun at one's testicles. It is also very awkward to reach with the weak hand, and difficult to conceal beneath a coat.

The draw is executed as with strong side, behind hip, but less shoulder rotation and "body English" are necessary.

Crossdraw. Conventionally, the crossdraw is worn on the hip opposite the gun hand, butt forward; in modern competition, the preferred position is "front crossdraw," with the holster closer to the navel than the hip, and tilted about 30°, both for a more natural grasp and to keep the barrel from digging into the leg when one sits.

The conventional crossdraw is banned from police competition and all but obsolete in uniformed police work, for several good reasons. At contact distance, an opponent can reach the weapon more quickly than the wearer. He could also jam your cross-reaching arm, something very difficult for him if, face to face, you reached for your straight-draw scabbard.

Starting at the opposite side of the body, the crossdraw gun sweeps wide with a pendulum effect that can easily swing it past its target. Finally, on the firing range, a gun coming out of a conventional crossdraw holster points its muzzle at those behind and beside the shooter.

Virtually all these problems are solved with the *front* cross-draw, worn at a 30° angle. By merely stepping forward with the weak side foot (or backward with the strong), the gun is placed in such a position as to be not only very awkward for an opponent to reach, but where your weak hand can push him away as you easily draw if he tries to block your hand.

Once the weak side is presented to the target, the shooter pulls the gun back and clear, then punches in forward toward the target. In this manner, it does not cross any other shooter and is quite safe for the range. It is also much faster; this is a directional draw that punches toward the target instead of sweeping across it. Once worn by Illinois State Police (during which ten year period no trooper was ever disarmed by an attacker), this style holster is favored by such speed champions as Mickey Fowler, John Shaw, Mike Dalton, and Bill Wilson.

For concealed street wear, the best front crossdraw is the Bianchi Belly-Band holster, which carries a 2" .38 revolver or small frame auto just to the left of the navel, under a tucked in shirt. Leave the second button above the belt undone (a necktie conceals the opening). The gun is now at midline of the body, and lightning-fast to reach.

Shoulder holsters. Most of us don't care to see upside-down shoulder holsters on the firing range, since on the draw, the muzzle crosses the range officer behind the shooter, the person on the shooter's left on the line, and often the shooter's own left arm. Still, under some types of clothing (i.e., a snugly-tailored dress suitcoat) a small gun in an upside down holster may be the best alternative. In addition to its other problems, however, the drawing motion tends to finish up with the gun at belt level instead of eye level, and one usually needs the front center of the coat open to reach the weapon.

A better shoulder holster is the conventional muzzle-down design, typified by the classic Bianchi X-15. Most people, however, don't know how to use it right. They tend to rip the gun all the way down through the open front of the holster, finishing up with the gun at belly level. This again requires a completely open coat. The gun is also pointed at people behind and beside you during the drawing stroke.

A better technique is to reach across the chest and grab the gun butt, then pull it up and out as if the holster were a pouch-type. Here again, you would want to stand with your weak side toward the target. Now, as the gun comes out across your chest, you just punch it straight toward the target... again, a safe draw that is also smooth and positive because it's directional.

This draw also allows you to clear the gun through a closed

outer garment of which only the top couple of buttons or few inches of zipper have been left open. It is particularly good in cold climates. And, unlike the conventional shoulder holster draw, the gun comes straight up and out along line of sight for maximum speed and accuracy.

NOTICE: A gun should *not* be worn in or on the belt on the strong side with the butt forward. While some find it slightly more concealable, this so-called "cavalry draw" causes the gun muzzle to cross your own lower torso during the draw. In a stress situation, there will be quite enough guns pointed at your vital organs without adding another one.

REHOLSTERING

The ability to holster the gun without looking at it is a mark of the master pistolero. This is also a necessary skill for those who may have to use the gun in a stress environment. When you re-holster, it may be dark, or you may have a crowd to keep your eyes on.

The latter situation comes about after you have captured a criminal at gunpoint and ordered him spread-eagled on the ground to await police. Unless you're wearing a blue uniform yourself, officers who arrive and see you with pistol in hand will find you doing a very convincing imitation of an armed criminal. They'll order you to drop the gun, which might now go off on impact (yes, some handguns will do that), or the bad guy may reach for it. Better the gun should be in your holster.

If you have to look at the holster to put it there, however, you're now in a blind sucker position and the first criminal, or a hidden accomplice in the gathering crowd, may choose to jump you. With your eyes on them and your hand still on the gun, however, you are an intimidating figure they're not likely to mess with . . . and when the police arrive, you just remove your hand from the holstered gun *very* slowly, announcing what you are doing.

The gun can be holstered one-handed by feel even if it has a safety strap. Insert the muzzle at the rear part of the holster opening, and rock the gun forward as you slide it into place. This way, it clears the leather strap. Obviously, you'll need a quality holster of rigid construction that will not close in upon itself from belt pressure or its own weight when the gun has been taken out of it. Notorious for this are the soft suede holsters that attach inside the waistband with metal clips. We in the trade call them "Fruit of the Loom" holsters.

If it occurs to you that it takes two hands to re-insert a gun in an upside down shoulder holster, you now see yet another reason why professionals are almost never seen wearing them.

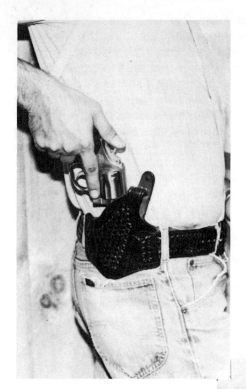

Proper Holstering 1: When gun is holstered by feel one-handed, a valuable combat skill for many reasons explained in text, thumb is on hammer holding it in position, and trigger finger is extended. This double-safes you against accidental discharge, and guides the gun into holster. Note that muzzle is inserted at angle "from back" . . .

Proper Holstering 2: . . . so that safety straps won't be in the way. Gun is now thrust home smoothly into holster. Hand may stay on it, or strap may be fastened, depending on situation. Practice while looking at it, then learn to do it by feel, one hand only.

Most quality holsters today are cut with the trigger guard covered. This is to prevent the finger from grabbing the trigger as the draw is begun, and accidentally shooting the wearer in the leg or buttocks. In this respect, the design has been successful.

Few realize, however, that such holsters also have a down side; if the finger is still on the trigger when the gun is holstered, the finger will catch at the edge of the leather and stop, while the gun keeps going. Congratulations: you have now shot yourself in the leg. I've personally seen two people "accidentally discharge" this way.

Since most police as well as civilian students at LFI are now using holsters with covered guards, I developed a new holstering technique for them. The finger is extended and thumb cocked upward, like a child playing cowboy. The thumb rests on the hammer, while the extension of the finger not only keeps it out of the trigger guard, but helps guide the weapon into the scabbard by feel. They call it the "index" finger for a reason. The thumb is a failsafe; if the index finger *has* caught on the leather and tripped the trigger, the thumb catches it in time to rectify the situation.

Chapter 7

StressFire Point Index

When the sights are used as the index of the weapon onto the target it is critical to keep visual focus on the front sight. When the eye focus wanders downrange to the target, the shooter misses — it's as simple as that, as any novice handgunner realizes.

But how does this relate to the proven fact that, in a gunfight, the Tunnel Vision Effect draws visual focus downrange to the source of the danger? The brutal answer is that this may be the single most important explanation of the Police Foundation study that reported that *of every four rounds fired by trained police officers in shootouts, only one hits the opponent anywhere!*

Since the FBI crouch, with its critical foot index, was not the answer, we looked elsewhere. What we came up with was the StressFire Sightpoint, an adaptation of the Point Shoulder firing position once taught by FBI.

FBI instructors taught the student to ignore the gun entirely, or to "look over" it. The trouble is that while the gun lines up in your lower peripheral vision in the calm atmosphere of the range, the much narrower field of view experienced within the Tunnel Vision Effect blots out the peripheral view of the weapon.

To correct this, we use only the front sight while thrusting the gun out ahead of the body, chest or shoulder high. A conscious effort is made to put that front sight on the opponent's body, though the rearsight is ignored.

A conventional sight picture looks like this:

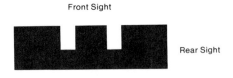

For some people, the StressFire Sightpoint looks like this:

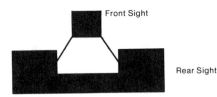

For most, including me, it looks like this:

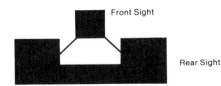

There is no one "sight picture" that works ideally for everyone. You have to play with it yourself and establish the proper coordinates for *you*. Arm length, neck length, distance between chest level and eye level, and even musculature of arms will make a difference. So will shape of face; oval faces have higher-placed eyes.

Here's how to tell which of the above sight pictures, or what one in between, will be right for you.

Using an UNLOADED gun AND a SAFE BACKSTOP THAT CAN CONTAIN BULLETS, practice thrusting the gun out in front of you at chest level while focusing on the target. Once the gun is out there and the hammer has dropped and clicked, *freeze everything but your head*. Now lower your head and, checking the sight picture, see where the bullet would actually have hit. (Have someone watching to make sure you don't also bend your knees, which throws the coordinates off.)

Repeat as necessary, until you've found a position where, with the gun in the lower periphery of your vision, it is in exact line with the target.

An alternative is to "backspace" that exercise, that is, to bend your head low and line the sights up on the target. Now freeze the gun arms, and lift your head erect, looking over the top of the gun and focusing on the target. The "over the top sight picture" you see either way is one you should memorize, because it will allow you to "point" the gun under stress and hit what you're aiming at while your eyes are focused downrange on the life-threatening target due to Tunnel Vision. This is because the gun is so close to eye level, you won't "lose it" in tunnel vision.

Once you've got your "visual index over the top of the gun" down pat during dry fire, it's time to practice it live, under safe conditions on the range. You'll find that very shortly, you can deliver close-range fire even more rapidly than if you were using the sights.

In close, the accuracy is astoundingly good. For the novice, accuracy drops off beyond 7 yards, and 10 yards is the practical limit. With practice though, 10 yards becomes a piece of cake, and 15 yards becomes functional. I've won "quick and dirty" IPSC freestyle combat matches using this technique at 15 yards, and use it routinely on the 10-meter "El Presidente" and "Vice Presidente" stages of IPSC competition.

At the eight-yard distances of the Second Chance profes-sional-class combat match, I've used this sight picture success-fully. So does Bill Byrd, who captured the overall championship with it one year. It's iffy, though; you're losing just enough in pure accuracy that you can hit off-center of that bowling pin target(see the author's book, "Hit the White Part," for a definitive guide to bowling pin shooting; it's available for $7.95 postpaid from Police Bookshelf, PO Box 122, Concord, NH 03301).

The trick is that you can *hit* five bowling pins more rapidly with the StressFire Sightpoint technique than you could in pure aimed fire. True, they may not be dead center . . . but a hit anywhere on a bowling pin at 8 yards equals a hit on a human being that would be in his heart, diaphragm, or spinal column for an almost certain "instant stop."

For man on man combat at close to intermediate range (under 15 yards for experts, under 7 to 10 yards for experienced shooters, under 5 yards for novices) the StressFire SightPoint is deadly fast and wickedly efficient. Most important, IT ALLOWS YOU TO VISUALLY INDEX THE SIGHTS EVEN THOUGH YOUR VISUAL FOCUS IS DOWNRANGE ON THE TARGET AS A RESULT OF TUNNEL VISION AND FIGHT OR FLIGHT REFLEX!

As ranges increase, you'll have to rely more on a classic sight picture and focus on your front sight. But as distances increase, you can afford to do that because distance favors the trained man in a shootout. The farther apart you are, the less the danger and the less your body experiences stress reaction. The problem is that most gunfights occur at ranges under 7 yards . . . and a substantial number of them are more like 7 *feet*.

In those close-range, down and dirty circumstances when tunnel vision and the other physio-psychological symptoms of gunfight stress kick into gear, the StressFire Point technique may be your best avenue to blasting the life-threatening danger into harmless, motionless silence.

And, needless to say, it also works well in the dark . . .

Chapter 8

The Punch Technique

Numerous approaches have been taken to one handed firing. The old FBI Crouch was one, and has been discredited as hopeless for most people to employ under stress.

Bill Jordan (author of the classic "No Second Place Winner" recommended one hand firing for speed as soon as the revolver had cleared its holster, moving nothing but the gun hand, a technique FBI was to adopt for close combat to replace the crouch some 16 years later. It is deadly fast and with considerable practice one learns a sort of "body index" for it, since there can be no visual index. Unfortunately, even Bill and the FBI agree that it's a very close range technique.

The problem is that all situations requiring a one handed shot may not conveniently be at point blank range. An awkward cover position ... a rescued child in one arm ... a gunshot injury through an arm or shoulder, may all keep you from firing two handed when the danger comes at 15 or 20 yards. In addition, the opponent may be on higher or lower ground, completely shattering your "felt index" in a hip shooting technique like the Jordan. I recall assisting another officer in the capture of multiple jail escapees under a bridge. One had picked up a fistful of sand to throw into the brother cop's face when I levelled my .357 one-handed from above him and barked a verbal command, ending the encounter.

The bridge was over a river. I was well above the escapee on the precipitously sloping riverbank, with my left hand holding a bridge strut for support. Had I gone to a two hand hold, I would have plunged into the river. Similarly, anything less than an arm's length hold would not have oriented the gun to the suspect so sharply below me, who it turned out was armed with a sharp screwdriver and within reach of attacking the other officer.

There is no ideal one hand technique. IPSC shooters, attempting to compensate for the tendency for the gun to point low in the close range Jordan method, developing a technique called the "speed rock"; the gun is fired as soon as it rocks out of the holster, and the torso bends back to straighten its angle. The problem is that the body is now completely off balance. Since this close range technique is most likely to be employed against a charging felon at point blank range, it is madness to totally break your body's balance before firing; in an instant he could be on top of you driving you helplessly to the ground.

Among extended arm techniques, one invariably finds weaknesses. The conventional marksman's position locks the arm, creating a fulcrum that lifts the gun sharply up and to the side, drastically slowing recovery time when follow up may be the difference between life and death.

The "instinct point" developed by Ray Chapman prevents this because the arm is sharply bent and acts like a shock absorber. Unfortunately, the gun is too far below line of sight to keep a visual index during the tunnel vision effect of extreme stress, the reason Chapman recommends it be used at no farther than four yards.

Another technique is to cant the pistol perhaps 30° toward your body. This lines up the joints in the arm more naturally and solidly, and for many will give a stronger hold and quicker recover time than any other locked arm position. It also takes getting used to, and the canting of the gun, at ranges of 25 yards and farther, alters point of impact on the target sufficiently to make a difference in proper placement and stopping effect.

Seeking a technique that would overcome these problems, I again looked to the martial arts. The technique I developed is called "the Punch."

The gun is brought up to line of sight (or just below it for a Stress Point Index) as if you were punching an opponent in the mouth or chin. The elbow is bent, not sharply, but just unlocked. Grip the gun tightly, and you will find that all muscles in the arm will tighten, thus maintaining a firm line of force behind the weapon. This couples with the shock absorber effect of the bent elbow to reduce felt recoil and snap even a Magnum or .45 immediately back on target. When shown next to locked arm techniques in the hands of the students themselves at LFI, the difference has been graphic and dramatic.

For maximum control of the gun, the body pivots at the pelvis as the gun is punched out. The "line of force" thus created travels from the rearmost foot, across the hips, through the shoulders and down the arm to the gun. *Without a firm hold and "line of force" control will be lost to the point that a wimpily held 44 Magnum could kick up and split your forehead open.*

Foot position is irrelevant. If your right foot happens to be back, it's a reverse punch (a blow delivered from the side of the body behind the lead foot); if the same foot is forward, its a forward punch; if both feet are planted equally, your knees will automatically flex slightly and lower your center of gravity as if you were punching from a "horse stance" in karate class. You shouldn't have to change foot position to execute "the punch."

A fellow student can watch to see if you're doing it right: the heel of the rearward foot will lift slightly. Don't try to do this consciously, however; the power comes from the pivot of the pelvis, and the rise of the heel is just a body dynamic that should happen without thought. Your fellow student should also be watching to make sure you don't hyperextend the arm and lock the elbow. The key to the technique is that it is a "pulled" punch. In kenpo and some other forms of karate, one is taught that the striking arm should never be fully extended, because power totally dissipates at the point of full extension. Remember the martial arts rule: a locked limb is a fulcrum of leverage that can be used against you, but a flexed limb is coiled power.

To prove this to yourself, square off with your wife or a smaller friend. Put their back against a wall and grab them by the collar with one hand, the elbow locked. If they place their palm gently a few inches above your elbow (no impact, please, or the joint will be broken), they can simply push sideways and almost effortlessly lever you away from them.

Now try it again, with the arm bent and exerting a line of force holding them against the wall. They will be unable to move you, because their power is being channelled uselessly into your arm. It is a simple Aikido technique, one that works quite well if you're grabbed on the street incidentally, but it illustrates the point that the flexed arm has much greater control of whatever it grasps than the locked arm.

Like the fellow student, your powerful handgun is fighting you. Either you'll control it, or it'll control you. Practicing the Punch technique will make you quickly able to deliver rapid accurate combat fire with a powerful handgun, and since the sights are brought up to eye level, the range of the technique is limited only by your own marksmanship.

Shortcomings? Because most Americans are used to holding their pistols fully at arm's length and to punching all the way to the

Punch 1: Standard one-hand firing position. Arm is locked, torso erect; shoulders are cantilevered back slightly to balance weight of gun. Accurate, but poor control for rapid combat fire with powerful gun.

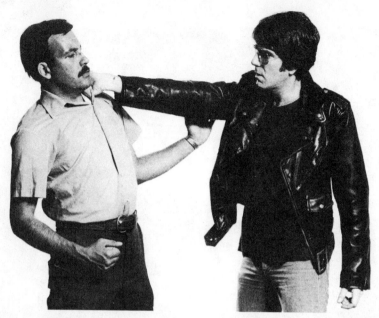

Punch 2: Here's the problem. David Price grabs author with locked arm, which becomes a fulcrum . . .

Punch 3: . . . and Ayoob easily throws locked arm (and Price) to the side. Fulcrum of locked arm allows pistol recoil to similarly "throw" your weapon off target.

Punch 4: This is the StressFire Punch technique. Arm is bent, creating recoil shock absorber effect. Hips have pivoted to throw gun forward; line of force extends from rear legs, up across hips, into gun arm. Note that rear heel has lifted from the ground. Body weight, and body force, are committed forward for much greater control.

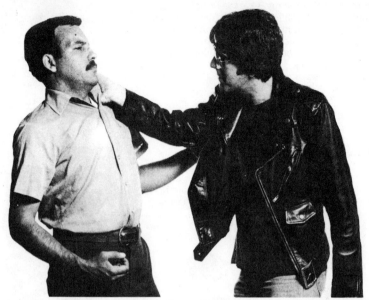

Punch 5: Price grabs author again, this time with bent arm and "line of force" punch technique, forcibly holding him away from himself . . .

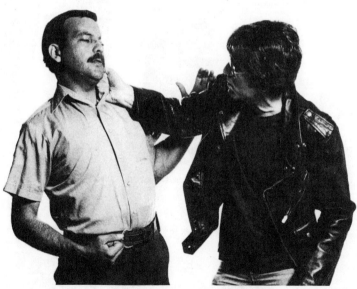

Punch 6: . . . and try as he might, author cannot dislodge him. Similarly, recoil of powerful gun when firing from this position is a resistance easily and quickly overcome.

Punch 7: StressFire Reverse Punch. Note that weak arm pulls back tight into body. This aids in momentum for shooting arm, and duplicates position of firing one handed on street (arm wounded, holding suspect or rescued victim).

Punch 8: StressFire Reverse Punch, seen from side. Note that line of force extends from rearward foot, across pelvis and shoulders, to gun hand. Arm is bent, but considerable body force is behind the gun, giving unmatched recoil recovery.

Punch 9: StressFire Forward Punch, so called because gun arm is on same side as leading foot. Don't step into the technique; fire from wherever you're standing. Just remember that line of force begins at rear foot.

Punch 10: StressFire Reverse Punch, seen from side. Note that upper body weight is forcefully committed forward to control recoil; bent elbow is "shock absorber" that makes gun kick straight back instead of upward.

end of the arms, it takes considerable practice to develop the "pulled punch" movement to instantly execute this technique and keep its shock absorber effect. I find that students of the classic Weaver hold adapt to the Punch more quickly, since they are used to shooting with their firing arm bent to the same slight angle. They notice that this technique improves recoil control much more in one handed shooting than in two handed firing.

If you do not wish to practice intensively on the technique, you can do fairly well with a locked arm if (a) you're not shooting anything harder kicking than a .38 revolver or a 9mm auto, and (b) you follow the other principles of the technique. These include:

1. Lean sharply forward to get the weight of shoulders and upper body behind the gun.

2. Pivot at the pelvis to get a line of force behind the weapon.

3. Bring your other arm up and lock the fist against your pectoral muscle. This is where the arm is likely to wind up anyway if you're shot (the "flipper effect" so often associated with a broken humerus bone) and also duplicates where the arm position would be if you were holding a rescued child. A bonus is that, as in the classic form of karate's reverse punch, pulling the opposite hand to this position gives more momentum to your upper body as you pivot into the technique and, therefore, increases the controlling power you have behind the gun.

The Punch technique with the bent arm is perhaps the one contradiction within the StressFire System, a subtle technique within a system designed for hard, positive, simple movements. I include it only because it is so dramatically superior to any other one hand method, one time an intentionally bent gun arm *is* going to be worth the effort to learn under stress.

Chapter 9

Weak Hand Shooting

The toughest thing to do with a handgun is fire it in your less dexterous hand. Yet this may be part of a worst case scenario, and you should train for it. Indeed, this training will make you a better shot in general by reinforcing good combat shooting habits, especially if you are an instructor.

I have twice had to carry and shoot left handed, due to hand injuries, once for a period of six months. During that time competing weak-handed, I was able to:

— Shoot the Chapman Academy's tough Advanced course successfully, often winning at least once on various stages while firing weak-handed-only;

— Win a PPC Automatic match against a man who had beaten me two previous times when I had shot strong handed, even though he shot his best score in that third match;

— Hold the man-on-man challenge event for more than two hours against all comers in an IPSC match;

— Beat virtually all comers, including the legendary Tom Campbell, in the "schoolhouse Exercise" phase of a night IPSC match.

Why? My left hand was a clean slate with no bad habits, and when I shot southpaw, I *had* to revert to basics and think, "solid hold, front sight, trigger squeeze." It taught me a lesson every instructor should share. Today, I don't consider a man a master instructor unless he owns a weak hand holster and at least once a year shoots a qualification or a match and/or teaches a class weak handed. I teach about one of ten classes with a left handed holster. It makes you prove that you know what you're doing, and it gives you, as an instructor, a feeling of what it is like for the worst student, who feels the gun to be a clumsy and alien presence in his hand.

Learning to draw weak-handed is another story. Whether you're reaching around the front or the back of your torso to a holster on what used to be your strong side, or whether you're drawing backwards out of a crossdraw, be sure the muzzle stays pointed away from your body and the bodies of others.

Weak-hand draw and reloading are discussed in more detail in my forthcoming book, "Gunfighting for Police: Advanced Tactics and Techniques." Suffice to say that you know you've reached a level approaching that of Master when you can hold your own shooting against your buddies in an informal match with your gun in your weak hand. While they're firing strong hand.

You will find that exotic one-handed techniques like the Punch will seem unnatural in your strong hand; that's because you've indoctrinated yourself, or been indoctrinated, to shoot another way. Your weak hand is a clean slate, however; you'll find that if you start your training with the Punch in your off hand, it will quickly become apparent that the technique is more natural than the conventional locked-out hold. Weak-hand firing is a good way to start your training with *any* new technique, since the realization that your left hand can master it overpowers the brain's subconscious feeling of "this ain't what we're used to," and allows you to open both your mind and your strong hand to a new and improved method of shooting that can improve your performance under stress.

Chapter 10

Concepts of Traversing

While I favor the locked arm Isosceles two hand hold as the basis of most stress combat shooting, I also drill my students on the Chapman and Weaver holds, largely to give them greater latitude in traversing their gun to the side. This will be necessary, because multiple opponents are likely to try to outflank you and also because you may be in a position such as the front seat of a car where you can't step around to "address" your target in your favorite stance.

The keys to traversing while standing are to leave the knees unlocked and to learn to pivot your body freely. Western man tends to be too "body-rigid" for his own good. Face your target at 12 o'clock with an Isosceles. Now turn slowly to your left without moving your feet (southpaws reverse). Notice that by the time you've gotten to 9 o'clock, your left elbow was involuntarily "broken" and bent; otherwise your movement would have jammed and stopped. As you get to about 7 o'clock, the strong arm bends too; go with it, because you're now in a classic Weaver. If your legs are flexed, you'll notice that they've bent more; were they locked, you would probably have lost your balance right now. A typical person can get all the way back to 180° with no problems so long as the knees flex to lower the pelvis for balance.

You'll notice that while you can feel the "40 pounds out, 40 pounds in" of isometric pressure between hands in this position, you don't have to think about it; the push pull is taken care of entirely by body torque! Notice also that the great shortcoming of the Weaver, the tendency for the strong arm to overpower the weak, doesn't happen here. *It can't*; the strong arm is now hyperextended and has maxed out on "push"!

Now swing back to your right, crossing 12 o'clock, and keep going. By the time you reach 3 o'clock your arms will again have locked into an Isosceles. Let the right elbow bend and you will find yourself going into sort of an "inside out Weaver" that lets you smoothly continue your traverse to about 4 or 5 o'clock. By lowering the pelvis and bringing the gun closer to your body you can learn to reach 6 o'clock comfortably. Just remember to keep pressing out with the gun hand. Where was it written that you couldn't fire with the weak arm straight and the strong arm bent? While not ideal, since it bends the shooting wrist (and could therefore jam an S&W 9mm or a too-finely-tuned Colt .45 auto) these techniques allow you to pivot smoothly in a way that allows you to literally cover 360° without moving your feet, so long as you keep your knees and arms flexed or ready to flex. You may find your toes pointing themselves automatically outward at times, but with this method there is never need for you to consciously move your feet unless you are extremely uncoordinated or have stiffness in your joints and pelvis.

You will be wanting to lean into the gun as much as possible, another reason to keep your knees flexible since if you were leaning the opposite way the powerful recoil of a hot .357 Magnum or a similar weapon could literally kick you backward. Most people find that to keep their balance they have to lean into the weapon anyway, which is all to the good.

Learning to incorporate the Isosceles, Chapman, and Weaver together are the mark of the true *pistolero*, and can save your life if you're ever caught in a narrow place or on extremely bad footing and have to engage a target at an awkward angle while unable to step into a better position.

Chapter 11

StressFire Kneeling

The kneeling position has a very real place in street combat shooting. It enables a winded, trembling shooter to fire from a more solid "base" on the ground, and more important, enables that person to take maximum advantage of low barricade cover. It is also useful when firing from behind a high barricade, especially if your first shots have been fired from a standing barricade position and drawn the opponent's attention to a relatively high point on the wall or obstacle you've taken cover behind.

Unfortunately, the great majority of combat pistol training uses an old kneeling position adapted from riflery: the suport elbow is bent, and braced on the knee. This may be helpful or even necessary with a 9 1/2 pound 7.62mm assault rifle. But it has numerous shortcomings in real-life combat pistol shooting. Anyone who can't hold their pistol steady without bracing an elbow on a knee is probably too physically feeble to be indulging in the sort of occupations or lifestyles that call for the carrying of defensive handguns.

The pure marksman not only braces elbow on knee, but often curls up his strong side foot under his buttock and actually sits on it. And, why not? On the FBI and NRA style combat courses standard with American police, one has 30 seconds to fire a mere six shots, and then reload for the next position.

And, in those matches or departmental qualifications, it is always safe to assume that no criminal is going to emerge from the side or on your flank and attempt to kill you . . . .

It's worth saying one more time: what works on the range or in the hunting fields, doesn't necessarily work on the street when you face multiple armed criminals intent on ambushing you from divergent angles and shooting you to death.

Let's examine that elbow on knee position which we'll henceforth call Marksman's Kneeling, point by point.

To get into it properly, you have to know exactly where you'll be facing your target. It is relatively slow to get into, and takes a lot of practice to learn to do quickly, with the elbow finding it's remembered "correct" position on the knee.

This position also "locks you up" and greatly restricts your ability to track a laterally running target, or to swing quickly on a new target that engages you from the side or flank.

Using empty hands, have a friend face you. "Aim" your non-existent weapon at him as if he was an antagonist, kneeling with your elbow braced on your knee. Now assume that a new antagonist has emerged on your right. Turn *quickly* and engage the imaginary foe. Notice how your arms seem to bind, and your body doesn't seem to be able to turn far enough, smoothly enough? Now engage a target on your left: it won't be as bad (if you're right handed), but you'll still find it very awkward.

The Marksman's Kneeling position tends to pull the gun in a bit too close to the face when engaging the target, and if you have to turn (especially to the strong side), it brings it even closer — *dangerously* close if you're using an autoloading pistol, the recoiling slide of which could easily strike you in the face as your reach becomes foreshortened with the turn.

One could attempt to remedy these problems by lifting the elbow off the knee when turning to engage a target other than the one originally lined up, but that's an unacceptably slow "change in the game plan" for someone to rely on under pressure in a life-threatening situation.

The Marksman's Kneeling position also does not take into account the fact that the officer might have to fire at an angle sharply above or below the flat piece of ground or pavement he may be kneeling on.

THE STRESSFIRE KNEELING POSITION answers these very real, street-oriented concerns.

In StressFire Kneeling, the shooter drops to the strong knee (right knee if right-handed) and *keeps the torso erect* with the arms thrust straight out in the Isosceles (Turret) position. He leans slightly forward.

From this position, the officer can instantly fire high or low, or "turret" to the left or right instantly without the torso muscles being bound up and stopped by a position that began with elbow on knee.

Let us assume the officer is down behind the engine block and

Marksman's Kneeling: Developed from rifleman's kneeling position, this technique is fine for target work but can be lethally unsuitable for gunfighting as author points out in text.

front wheels of his patrol car in a cover position. Unless he is very tall, the elbow-on-knee position won't permit him to aim over the car hood to return fire: the StressFire position will. The writer is 5'10" tall and finds only a few inches of vertical adjustment possible with the elbow-on-knee position. I have about two and a half *feet* of vertical adjustment (from a deep "kneeling crouch" to kneeling with the torso fully erect and pelvis high) using the StressFire Kneeling position. This allows much more real-life flexibility for taking advantage of a variety of cover points when returning fire.

With the StressFire Kneeling position and the arms held in an Isosceles, try again the trick of aiming your EMPTY HANDS at a partner or imaginary target straight in front of you (12 o'clock). Now engage to your left (9 o'clock). Now, engage to your right (3 o'clock). Do you notice the almost complete freedom of movement?

Less is sacrificed with StressFire Kneeling in terms of accuracy than anyone realizes. Indeed, Frankie May of the NYCPD Firearms Training Unit used an early version of this position to win multiple NRA National Police Combat Championships: he swore that the pistol being further extended from his eyes gave better "eye relief" and more precise accuracy. (That would be even more true for an officer with corrective lenses, who would often not be looking through the optically correct "center of his prescription" in a hastily taken elbow-on-knee kneeling position, or who might even be looking out over the tops of the lenses. The same is true for the older officer wearing bifocals who needs his head upright and perhaps even tilted slightly back if he is to get a good sight picture through the lower "reading" half of his split lenses.)

This writer has won state and regional championship events, and set two national records, using the StressFire Kneeling position, and won numerous lesser matches with it. It sacrifices little or nothing on the range . . . and on the street, it can save your life.

Remember once more that on the street you're in a fight and need to maintain your balance and your mobility. It is critical that as you kneel, your foot on the kneeling side contact the pavement with the BALL of the foot. Instep-down or sitting on the edge of the shoe may be fine in a combat match, but on the street won't give you the leverage to quickly change positions or spring to your feet to reach a new cover point in the heat of a shootout.

Knee position isn't nearly as critical in the StressFire technique as it is with Marksman's Kneeling, but even so, you want to practice for ideal mobility. Assume that as you face the opponent, you are standing on a giant clock dial with the opponent at 12 o'clock. As a right handed man drops to his right knee he wants that kneecap splayed out to about 2 o'clock, with his upraised left knee pointing to about 11 o'clock. Make that "10 and 1 on the clock" for the left-hander.

StressFire Kneeling 1: Torso is upright, arms are fully extended in front of body with no attempt to mate elbow on knee. Note that upright body better adapts to low barricade cover like auto hood. Ball of right foot is on ground; right-handed man's right knee is down.

StressFire Kneeling 2: Opponent's eye view of StressFire Kneeling. Balance is superior to conventional "high kneeling" or "Frankie May" position, since left knee is out to 11 o'clock and right knee at 2 o'clock. Note also that center of balance can be lowered (buttock to heel) to adjust for low cover.

This turns the body into a close-to-the-ground tripod whose low center of gravity greatly stabilizes the shooter's body as a "gun platform." The points of the tripod are the weak foot (flat), the strong knee, and the ball and toes of the strong foot.

In this position, the shooter can afford to lower his buttock onto his strong heel, still further increasing stability. This forces the torso *slightly* forward, which is no problem: indeed, leaning into the weapon this way helps control rapid high power recoil and better balances the shooter to leap to his feet if movement is required.

It takes only minutes of practice to see why the StressFire Kneeling position is superior in every way to the conventional "braced kneeling" positions. It is quicker to get into and quicker to get out of. It is much more widely adaptable to a variety of barricade cover positions. It does not reduce combat accuracy. Finally, and perhaps most important, it gives the shooter a much greater latitude for engaging multiple targets that may appear by surprise on his flank.

Indeed, the StressFire Kneeling position is the basis for the one combat firing position in which you can engage opponents on a full 360° without moving your feet — a technique we call the StressFire Star.

Chapter 12

The StressFire Star

Be honest: Do you or do you not think it is impossible to teach someone in only a few minutes to be able to fire at any point 360° around them from a kneeling position without consciously moving their feet?

I didn't think it was possible either until I developed the StressFire technique.

Because I so strongly advocated use of cover and because tactical training and review of actual street gunfights had made me acutely aware of the danger of being outflanked, I sought a technique that would allow a shooter kneeling behind cover to return flanking fire to any point on the 360° compass.

From the kneeling position, any of the conventional pivot-strike techniques were out, at least for covering the whole circle. An alternative taught by some was for the shooter to fling himself to his back and fire upside-down at the opponent who had outflanked him. That awkward, unnatural technique is best left for the wounded officer already put on his back by hostile fire.

Once again, I found the answer from my years on the martial arts scene. That answer had been there all the time; it was just that no one who taught the pistol had ever studied its use in terms of the principles of Aikido, the subtle Japanese art whose name means "the way of the spirit moving."

The technique is ridiculously simple, and is learned in seconds. Aikido practitioners call it "the star," and it is a basic fundamental for students of the art. They merely do it with empty hands.

Imagining a pistol in your hand, take a StressFire Kneeling position, with your left leg up at 11 o'clock and your right knee on the ground pointing to 2 o'clock, assuming that your initial target is at 12 o'clock and you're right-handed.

Engage to your left (9 o'clock). Depending on your upper body shape and musculature, you may still be in the Isosceles position or your weak elbow may already have bent into a Chapman position as your gunsights lock on at 9 o'ckock.

Turn farther to your left. As the pistol comes into line between 8 and 7 o'clock, the strong elbow involuntarily bends into a Weaver hold. Lock there: you'll feel that the 40 pounds out, 40 pounds inward pressure is being exerted on the pistol between your hands, but you don't have to consciously apply that pressure the way you do in a conventional, standing Weaver Hold. The right arm, now hyperextended, can no longer overpower the left as so often happens with the conventional Weaver.

A very flexible person with a good sense of balance may even be able to turn and engage directly behind himself at 6 o'clock, but most people will be strained and off balance if they attempt to push it that far.

Return now to your original hold on the target at 12 o'clock in the original StressFire Kneeling position. Engage now to your right, at 3 o'clock. Depending again on your upper bodyshape, you may already have forced your elbows to bend into a modified Weaver position. but if you attempt to turn farther to your right flank from here, you'll find it extremely awkward, uncomfortable, and unnatural.

Thus, merely pivoting the hips in the StressFire Kneeling position, while giving you vastly more flexibility and latitude of return fire coverage than the conventional kneeling position, still leaves you with an area from approximately 3 o'clock to 7 o'clock on your right flank exposed.

With the Star, the solution is as simple as two words.

Change knees.

That's right, change knees. As your torso pivots on the gunmount axis of the hips, your weak knee drops to the ground and your strong knee rises.

This instant rearrangement of the lower body "tripod on the ground" instantly frees you to sweep immediately around to your right in an Isosceles hold, and cover completely the area behind you! The movement is swift and natural, perfectly balanced as is virtually everything in Aikido . . . and it gives you an instant coverage of 360° around you with your handgun in an extremely solid return fire position!

The Star technique works moderately well with both knees down, but most will find it much more flexible and natural with the

StressFire Star 1: Star was adapted by Ayoob from Aikido technique for turning 360° plus from kneeling. One begins facing target at 12 o'clock in StressFire Kneeling . . .

StressFire Star 2: . . . from here, shooter can turn to 9 o'clock. Weak arm will want to bend; *let it*, and flow naturally into a Chapman hold. Note that body rises as it turns toward weak side . . .

StressFire Star 3: . . . as body turns to about 7 or 8 o'clock and reaches maximum extension, torso and pelvis have risen, and arms have bent into Classic Weaver. Note that here, as in S.F. Reverse to Weaver Pivot-Strike, strong hand can no longer overpower weak hand in Classic Weaver...

StressFire Star 4: Sweeping back across 12 o'clock and continuing clockwise, arms go back into Isosceles. Body binds between 2 and 3 o'clock, so left knee starts to drop then . . .

StressFire Star 5: ...and left knee drops to ground while right knee lifts. Torso is now free to continue traverse to 4 or 5 o'clock...

StressFire Star 6: ... and with hip and torso again lifted, gun can freely traverse to 7 or 8 o'clock, giving 360° plus of coverage. Author has taught this technique in one to two minutes on range to hundreds of students, should obviously not be done live fire on conventional range.

strong-side knee only on the ground. In the martial arts, the concept of the Aikido Star is more involved and requires more foot movement; for combat shooting, the above is all you need and doesn't get you into the complex foot movements that anyone but an advanced, highly practiced expert would find awkward in the stress of a firefight.

The Stressfire Star is easily remembered: It is simply the StressFire Kneeling position with knee position reversing as the turn becomes acute. *Notice that no conscious movement of the feet is required.*

At the outset of this chapter, how many of you thought it *was* impossible to cover a full circle from the kneeling position without moving your feet or firing between your legs like a trick shooter? If you doubt the simplicity and functionability of the StressFire Star it is because you haven't tried it yet.

NATURALLY, THE STRESSFIRE STAR, LIKE ANY OTHER FORM OF LIVE SHOOTING AT VARIOUS ANGLES, SHOULD BE PRACTICED ONLY ON A SPECIAL RANGE WITH 360° BULLET ABSORBENCY AND WITH ALL OTHER SHOOTERS TOTALLY BEHIND SUFFICIENTLY PROTECTIVE COVER.

This caveat does not, however, limit learning to those people who have a "maze" range, "funhouse range", or tristeelwalled partition. I've taught it to classes of more than 25 in as little as two minutes. The key is that in this sort of training NO GUNS ARE USED AS THE STUDENTS PRACTICE THEIR TURNS. Later, on the controlled range, they may fire from each point on the StressFire Star under the watchful gaze of the training officer, who makes sure that the gun muzzles never pan other participants in, or observers of, the training exercise.

Chapter 13

Pivot Strikes

Danger often comes from behind, giving you no opportunity to "address your target" like a classic marksman; it's turn quick and fire, or die.

Most of the marksmanship academies teach only one manner of dealing with this situation (if any), and I've only seen one other school, Chapman Academy, show two or more. At LFI, we show six techniques the student may adapt as needed to his own physique. Instructors going through our police program are required to learn all six, so they too can adjust the techniques to their students.

FBI Pivot. The first such technique was adapted by the FBI, after they realized their crouching hip shooting didn't work worth a damn unless the feet were indexed with where the opponent was standing. To execute the technique, one pivots on the holster side leg, so the weapon will not be pulled away from the reaching hand.

The pivot can move to any necessary degree, but is limited by the dexterity and coordination of the shooter. It doesn't allow for last-moment adjustments.

One would turn, say, to three o'clock by kicking forward off the weak leg; to do a 180° turn, one would kick backward (to the right handed man's left) for greater power. However, one may occasionally stumble, since stopping a rearward movement with the heel, as happens with this technique, leaves little room for balance adjustment. Still, the technique is quickly and easily learned by most people.

About-Face. Developed for IPSC shooting and promulgated by

FBI Pivot 1: In the FBI pivot, you turn on the holster-side leg, kicking *back* with the opposite leg . . .

FBI Pivot 2: . . . pivoting on the ball of the holster-side foot toward the target . . .

86

FBI Pivot 3: . . . and finish in a combat hold, 1 or 2 handed.

Jeff Cooper at the famous Gunsite, where it is still taught at this writing, the about-face is a deadly fast technique for doing 180°, though it is practically limited to that degree of movement and is not well suited to only partial turns.

To execute, one steps the weak foot behind the strong foot, and then simply pivots on the balls of the feet. It is quick, but the crossing of the ankles breaks the balance, excessively so for very tall or wide-bodied people. Also, like the FBI Pivot, it's a good way to cause a bad fall if executed on a staircase, ice, or broken ground.

Chapman Turn. With his practiced eye for human physiology, world champ Ray Chapman developed the method of beginning the turn by throwing the gun-side shoulder forward, thus quickly gathering upper body momentum for speed and power. As the body surges around, the strong side foot, which has begun to step, drives itself solidly into the ground. Because body momentum is going forward instead of back, the impact lands on the foot and goes through the most flexible part of the leg, making the technique virtually stumble-proof and also allowing last instant adjustments, making it in both ways superior to the FBI Pivot. People are also less likely to lose their balance than with the about-face technique.

Fast and positive, the Chapman Turn has only one drawback: if the holster is worn on the strong side, the weapon is moving away from the reaching hand. A good execution of this technique, therefore, requires a seasoned shooter with excellent hand-to-holster coordination.

StressFire Pivot Strike #1. The Rescue Turn. The fastest method of getting a shot off at an attacker behind you may be simply to turn to the right if you're right handed, shove the damn gun out, and fire. Shortcomings are obvious: even though it's extremely fast, you're firing with only one hand, and the fact that the arm will usually lock when thrust behind you increases the recoil effect and slows recovery time between shots. Also, if the attacker was at a point blank range, he might be able to grapple for the gun, since you can't protect it with the other hand as in most of the other pivot-strike techniques.

The raison d'etre of the Rescue Turn is in its name. Teaching civilians to protect their homes with guns, we at LFI had taught them to take their small children from their beds to the master bedroom if the home was invaded. But what if they were attacked during that moment?

The Rescue Turn allows you to fire one-handed while holding an infant (or, if you insist, your Krugerrands) in your other hand. Your body is between the child and the opposing gunfire. Naturally, we want something to be between *you* and the opposing fire, too; the technique was tailored to work well for a man wearing soft body

Cooper Turn 1: Taught by Jeff Cooper and widely used in IPSC, this is simply a military about-face . . .

Cooper Turn 2: . . . weak-side foot steps around behind gun side foot (preferably *way* around) . . .

Cooper Turn 3: . . . turns on the balls of the feet as the hands meet in a Weaver hold . . .

Cooper Turn 4: . . . and finished in a Weaver stance.

90

Chapman Turn 1: Inspired by IPSC ace Tom Campbell, the Chapman turn begins with hands in any position . . .

Chapman Turn 2: . . . The shoulders surge around toward weak side, carrying body with them as hand goes for pistol . . .

Chapman Turn 3: . . . as hands take their position and target comes into sight, trailing rearward foot is driven back . . .

Chapman Turn 4: . . . and body is slamlocked into position on target. Chapman stance is shown; technique is adaptable to other stances, as are Cooper and FBI pivots.

armor. Notice that, from the rear, the side has not been distinctly presented to the opponent, and the ballistic shield is still protecting most or all major internal organs.

The Rescue Turn, while sacrificing some degree of shooting ability with the one locked gun arm, gains in the above areas and also in that it is a very well balanced position which can be executed on virtually any footing. Practice it holding an object of appropriate weight, or at least, with your weak arm drawn up to the pectoral muscle.

You may also wish to practice starting with your face to the target, then turning to get your "cargo" between it and your armored body before you fire.

StressFire Pivot Strike #2. Pivot to Kneeling. Actually the first of the StressFire pivot strikes, this one was developed to answer the need for something that would work on stairwells and other uneven surfaces. It is simplicity itself: drop to the right knee and turn to your left if you're right handed. You'll come up in a solid kneeling position, your arms in either a Chapman or Weaver hold, your body now a gun platform — a tripod mounted low to the ground, where an instant ago you were an awkward, erect biped.

If you're going upstairs or uphill and have to turn to deal with someone below, you may find yourself leaning slightly against the ground or stairs; this will only increase your solidity. If you have to turn while moving downstairs, make sure your strong-side leg is ahead; otherwise, you can lose your balance.

Downside? Very heavy people may over balance when suddenly lowering their center of gravity and turning simultaneously, and it's obviously not going to work if you have bad knees. Practice on a soft surface, and if you want to work on stairs, do us both a favor and start on the *bottom* step with a safe-fall area behind you until you've mastered the technique and made sure it works for your particular body.

StressFire Pivot Strike #3. Reverse to Weaver. Possibly the simplest of all the techniques presented here, and among the most useful. Without moving the feet consciously, simply pivot at your waist and come up into a Weaver hold. Since the body is torqued, it will hold the bent arms with equal isometric tension without your having to think about it.

You *will* need to have your knees unlocked; the way the body maintains balance in this movement is to flex the knees, lowering center of gravity as the turn becomes deeper. You won't have to think about this; just turn, and your body will do it for you. You can see it yourself if you have someone photograph, or better yet, videotape you while practicing. Videotape is one of the greatest training aids and to ever come down the pike. I or Ray Chapman or

StressFire Pivot Strike 1: StressFire technique is the only pivot-strike that works on stairs. Here, author is moving upward . . .

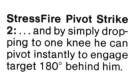

StressFire Pivot Strike 2: . . . and by simply dropping to one knee he can pivot instantly to engage target 180° behind him.

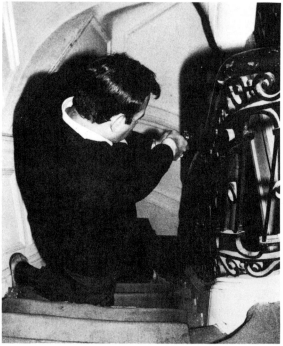

StressFire Pivot Strike 3: Technique works the other way on stairs. Sensing movement behind him as he walks downstairs, Ayoob places right foot on lower step . . .

StressFire Pivot Strike 4: . . . and again drops to right knee as he pivots to engage. Note extremely solid balance, low center of gravity with both Stress-Fire techniques.

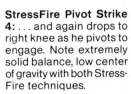

StressFire Rescue Pivot 1: For the individual carrying a child or dragging injured adult from danger scene, who must engage attacker from behind.

StressFire Rescue Pivot 2: Weak arm is pulled into upper body (simulates holding toddler) and knees flex deeply as gun is drawn. This is the only technique where one should do pivot strike clockwise if right-handed.

StressFire Rescue Pivot 3: Gun arm is extended one-handed, shooter looking out of corner of eye. This keeps maximum body armor between shooter and opponent, though main purpose is to keep armor between opponent and victim being rescued. For rescue of adult, drop to kneeling.

StressFire Pivot to Kneeling 1: Designed by Ayoob for execution on stairways, ice, broken ground, or other uncertain surfaces.

StressFire Pivot to Kneeling 2: As gun is drawn, shooter turns toward weak side (counter-clockwise for right handed man) and drops to right knee.

StressFire Pivot to Kneeling 3: . . . From this kneeling position, body can naturally take a Classic Weaver aiming at point 180° behind shooter.

StressFire Reverse to Weaver 1: For use when the shooter cannot change foot position yet must engage behind him, i.e., when trapped between two closely-parked vehicles.

StressFire Reverse to Weaver 2: As shooter draws, he turns toward his weak side, i/e/, right handed man turns to his left. the *knees flex deeply* . . .

StressFire Reverse to Weaver 3: . . . and shooter is in a crouch from the waist down, a Classic Weaver from the waist up. Difficult for the obese and stiff, but surprisingly natural for the average person. *Lean into gun* to absorb recoil; warns Ayoob, who developed technique.

Jeff Cooper could tell you all day that you're doing something right or wrong, but when you can actually see yourself do it, the lesson is instantly slammed home.

The reverse-to-Weaver works very well for most people, but is contra-indicated for those with bad backs or bad joints, or extreme weight problems. Weaver stance purists need not fear that the unlocked knees will spoil their technique. True, some have been conditioned by instructors who rap their kneecaps with a riding crop if they bend their knees. In fact, however, Jack Weaver originally shot with his knees bent; it was Jeff Cooper who brought in the locked legs, for the very good reason that locked legs make a better firing platform in pure marksmanship. Obviously, marksmanship and gunfighting do not always coincide in their principles. I understand that Smith & Wesson Academy teaches the Weaver with slightly unlocked legs.

Will you need to master all six pivot strikes? Not unless you're an instructor. I find the three Stressfire techniques neatly bracket about everything you'll need to turn and fire for on the street: Protecting a loved one (technique #1), turning on ice or snow or stairs (technique #2), or instant speed response at varying distances (technique #3). For competition, where the match is always going to be on level ground, I would go with the Chapman Turn or the About Face; the StressFire techniques, having been designed for the street, might allow the muzzle to cross the spectators in a tournament unless you were working from a crossdraw holster.

Chapter 14

Getting Low and Solid

The rationale of prone shooting has always been two-fold: to make you a smaller target, and to give you the most solid possible firing position. The trouble is that, in attempting to achieve both those noble purposes, it was taught wrong for decades, and often still is.

FBI discovered in the late 1960's that if a bullet hit a flat surface in front of you at an angle of 40° or less, it was likely to "skip" and come straight at you within one to eight inches of the ground. Also, FBI and their police instructor proteges around the nation taught prone in a rigid position perpendicular to the target, belly down and feet together, to minimize target exposure. Unfortunately, this awkward position placed great strain on the neck and forced most people to raise their hands off the ground to see the sights, thus destroying the inherent accuracy of what should be a wonderfully solid technique.

Both problems were solved with the advent of the rollover prone technique. Developed by Ray Chapman in the early days of IPSC, and promulgated by Jeff Cooper long before Chapman began teaching, the rollover is comfortable, solid, and superbly adaptable to use behind cover. Even FBI went to it, in 1981.

Roll onto your gun hand side, with your body at about a 45° angle to your target, your feet to the left if you're right handed, and your left knee drawn up. You may optionally cross your left foot onto the back of your right knee, though you'll get to your feet again a little quicker if you don't.

Thrust the gun arm straight to the target, and bring the hand up to support. The contact point with the ground should be the heel of the weak hand. Rest your chin or cheek on shoulder or bicep — you'll have to find your own index, because everyone's face, neck, and arms are of different dimensions — and you should be ready to go. You'll know it's right when you can let your body go dead in total relaxation with no muscles being tensed except those in the hands, yet the sights are on target. If it doesn't feel right, move more over onto your right ribcage or extend your legs up to a more sharply inclined angle, more parallel with the firing line or protective wall.

That's for a right handed man shooting around a right-side wall. For a left side wall, use a mirror image and, still keeping the gun in your strong hand, cock the wrist until the weapon bears on target. An alternative is to switch the gun to the weak hand, especially if your gun is a 9mm. Smith & Wesson, a target-tuned .45, or other auto that will only cycle reliably with the shooting wrist locked.

While the straight-on, old-fashioned police prone position would have left half your body exposed to enemy gunfire, this technique allows most of your body to stay behind cover.

With his technique, Chapman developed a method of getting into it fast that beats anything anyone has come up with since. While some of the young Turk IPSC shooters simply fling themselves to the ground and let fly, that technique only works on nice, soft, well-mowed firing ranges. On broken ground or in an alley, you could drive a broken bottle through your chest or land on a rock and puncture your liver with a broken rib going prone like that. The Chapman technique is protective enough for street or forest use.

If you're going down into the standard rollover position with the target at 12 o'clock, turn your body to 2 o'clock before you start to move. Draw your gun, and keep it safely ahead of you, finger off trigger and safety engaged.

Drop to both knees, your gun hand going out toward the target and your left palm falling to the ground to catch your weight. As it does, slide the gun hand along the ground toward the target (you'll want to be wearing something with sleeves to prevent abrasions) as your torso now lands on the ground, the impact having been cushioned by left palm and right forearm. Now, bring the support hand up into firing position and tuck up the left leg. You should soon be able to go from standing start to killing hit at 50 meters with this technique in three seconds.

SPEED SITTING

The sitting technique, still used at 50 yards in police competition and some police training, is all but useless in combat. You won't be

Prone 1: Author lectures students on shortcomings of standard police prone position, demonstrated by LFI instructor Rick Devoid.

Prone 2: Police prone: ankles together makes for poor lateral body stability; gun has to be lifted off ground to see sights, ruining stability; head is tilted back, causing tension, discomfort, and distorted visual perspective for corrective lens wearers. Moreover, if Rick was firing from behind cover, half of him would be exposed to enemy fire.

Prone 3: In rollover prone, gun hand is braced solidly on ground and body is utterly stable. Only gunhand and part of head would be exposed from behind cover. A superior position in every way.

105

Prone 4: Relay of LFI students taking first run on rollover prone. Two in center have had to raise their guns because they're lying on their bellies instead of their sides. Position was first developed by Ray Chapman, first taught by Jeff Cooper, and adopted by FBI in 1982.

Prone-Out 1: Author uses Chapman Method for getting prone. Facing the target (12-o'clock) he turns his body to 2 o'clock. Knees begin to bend. Gun is drawn (from shoulder holster) and pointed in direction of target; finger is off trigger and safety is on.

Prone-Out 2: Ayoob drops to knees, and weak hand goes forward to catch his upper body weight, staying clear of gun muzzle. Trigger is still untouched, safety still "on".

Prone-Out 3: As left hand catches, torso goes to ground and gun slides forward to target. Force of movement may often throw left foot in the air.

Prone-Out 4: Author has let foot fall across back of knee, a Cooper modification that is very stable. Support hand has come up, cheek rests comfortably on bicep, and firing commences.

Weak Side Rollover Prone: When right-handed man has to fire prone around a left side wall, use mirror image position. Most teach placing gun in weak hand, but author finds cocking wrist of strong hand, as shown, works better. Feet are apart in the original Chapman version of the rollover prone position.

sitting to shoot unless you're caught behind a desk or a dashboard when it goes down, and your best advice there is to dig in your feet, lean forward, and fire.

I developed the speed sitting technique for two reasons. First, when I was an active competitor in, and sponsor of, PPC matches I noted from the control tower that in most tournaments, there would be an average of 13 seconds from when the start signal went off, to when the first shot was fired on the fifty yard line (most 50-yard PPC shooting begins with the sitting position, going then to prone and left and right standing barricades).

Also, I had found as a handgun hunter that even if one was on a stand, one usually wasn't in a position to use a tree as a support for a long shot, and if you went prone, all you were going to see was weeds and bushes as the deer scampered merrily off. Sitting position was almost as solid, and kept you high enough to see over the brush. Now if I could only do it *quick* . . .

The sitting positions are the most varied you'll ever see on a firing line, from leaning back on one elbow and balancing the gun one handed on a knee, to wrapping both arms around a knee and leaning back to let the torso hang precariously over the buttocks, to almost anything imaginable. Most positions either compressed the viscera and made breathing and steady hold difficult, or made the hold wobbly; all were slow to get into. The technique I had developed by 1973, when I won the New Hampshire State PPC Championship with it, got past all those shortcomings.

As you take the firing line (or when you see the deer), assume that the target is at 12 o'clock and turn your left hip to about 7 o'clock. Cross your left foot behind your right foot, letting the knees touch for index and stability. Draw the gun and point it downrange, finger off trigger and safety "on".

Let the left palm fall to the ground and take your weight as your knees bend. Lower the body until the left hip touches the ground, then roll your butt onto the deck. Your ankles are crossed; leave them that way and lock them. Bring your right arm, locked, across your right knee, taking a firm Wedge hold on the pistol. The arms are ideally locked out in an Isosceles for maximum stability. The left elbow is across the left knee.

The torso should now be erect, leaning neither forward nor back, and properly balanced so that you can breathe and don't have to struggle to stay upright. The arms are braced across the tripod formed by the two feet and the buttocks at either end of the bent legs (more of a quadrupod, actually).

If you are heavy around the middle and find this cramped, you may wish to lean back slightly. This will be facilitated by something like a canteen on the middle of your belt in the back, to lean against

Speed-Sitting 1: Ayoob developed this technique for competitive shooting and hunting, where he has used it successfully. He offers it for those purposes, *not* gunfighting.

Speed-Sitting 2: As hand goes to holstered gun, weak foot crosses behind strong-side foot. Simultaneously, weak hand is extended downward.

Speed-Sitting 3: Weak hand catches body weight as buttocks roll onto the ground. Feet are already in crossed-ankle position.

Speed-Sitting 4: Sitting position is almost complete; ankles lock as weak hand comes up to support.

Speed-Sitting 5: Hand meets hand, forearms are rigidly supported across tops of ankle-locked knees, and superb balance is almost instantly achieved.

and provide lumbar support. PPC shooters used to put double speedloader pouches there for just that reason, until it was ruled illegal in competition.

With a bit of practice, you'll find it no trick to go from standing start to solid sitting position in three seconds. We emphasize again that this technique is for hunting and PPC match shooting, not combat. It remains the fastest sitting technique yet developed and possibly also the most stable. We do not apologize to combat gunners for its inclusion here; anyone who doesn't think sport shooters need stress techniques has never looked across his gunsights at a whitetail deer, or at a target in a big-money match. I've done both . . . and speed sitting has worked for me.

Chapter 15

Dark StressFire

It is a fact that most shootouts occur in dim light. It is equally true that they occur suddenly with very little time to take recourse to a glow-in-the-dark Nite Site or T-Sight. There are some who'll tell you that night shooting is the ultimate *raison d'etre* for learning instinct shooting . . . if, of course, you believe that there is such a thing as instinct shooting.

There is no human instinct to shoot in the dark, to manipulate the mechanical object that is the firearm and propel its little pellet where you wish it to go. Mechanical weapons like firearms came along too late in the epoch of the human experience for instinct to catch up with the requirements of indexing them in the dark.

But suppose we told you that we could teach you a "radar" system of automatically locking in via sound to a target in the dark, locking in so unmistakably that you could shoot it with almost 100% certainty even if you couldn't see it, at close combat distance?

I was skeptical too, until we saw NYPD's success with the basic version, completed our advanced experiments, and began teaching it a few years ago. The ability does exist. It's a piece of cake. But I can't teach it to you.

I can only awaken you to it.

That's because you already possess it . . . .

There is no "instinct" to crouch low and thrust the gun out in front of you, as in the old FBI technique. There is no "instinct" to bend your left arm a lot and your weak arm a little with 40 or 45 pounds of isometric tension on the gun in between as you kick off with your weak leg and try to come down on line with your target in a Weaver hold. But there *is* an instinct to do something else.

If you're a parent, you remember how obsessed you were with the development of your children, at least your firstborn. You remember leaning over the cradle of the newborn infant just home from the hospital nursery. You remember speaking to it or tapping your hand against the side of its crib.

And the child looked directly at you.

Pediatricians tell us that within the first week or two of birth the child cannot focus its eyes and they're not sure if it even "sees" anything as adults perceive "sight." But you made that sound and the child looked, its eyes and head focused on the source.

So did you, in your first week as a living human organism, and that has been with you forever after. When you hear a sound in the dark you look at it, and all the time you've been alive you've learned to coordinate your eyes with your ears. Have you not found that almost always, even before you actually see and before you even realized you were doing it, you are looking at what made that noise in the dark?

That reflex can keep you alive in a night shootout, but only if it is properly channelled. If you look at the noise and get a visual lock on the gunman who is stalking you, it won't do you any good if now you have to try to execute an FBI Pivot to line your feet up exactly right with the danger point and fire from waist level. It won't do you a whole lot more good if you have to kick off with your weak leg and hope to God that your hands remember the exact isometric coordinates that line your Weaver hold in the dark *once the visual index of the sight picture is obscured by night.*

But suppose your arms were already locked into the Isosceles Turret position. And now suppose that you have taken the one additional step of Dark StressFire: YOU HAVE LOCKED YOUR NECK AS WELL AS THE REST OF YOUR BODY ABOVE THE CHEST.

Now, with your upper body locked, your eyes turn toward the danger with that life long instinct — AND WITH THEM TURN THE HANDGUN ALREADY LOCKED ON TARGET! WHAT YOUR EYES SEE IS NOW AUTOMATICALLY COVERED BY YOUR SIDEARM!

Naturally, YOU NEVER FIRE AT A TARGET YOU HAVE NOT IDENTIFIED AS ONE YOU SHOULD SHOOT AT. Yet the time saving, and the instinctive lock, are obvious. You really have to try it on the range to believe how effective it is.

Even if you have failed to lock the neck, Dark StressFire still works. Once you have turned, your visual focus will instinctively lock onto the danger source that alerted you: BRING YOUR WEAPON UP THEN INTO AN ISOSCELES HOLD and it will be locked on target! With the Isosceles Turret you still need not worry, even at this late point, about using your feet as coordinates to index you in the dark. Your feet will find their own balance, as they, too, have been doing for you all your life.

Even in total darkness, Dark StressFire will allow you to shoot with great effectiveness. Few shootings occur in pitch blackness: virtually all of the 6,000 armed encounters NYPD documented in 10 years were in situations where there was enough ambient light to identify the opponent and point or aim the gun at him. In those circumstances, Dark StressFire is ideal, allowing a last-instant visual verification of sight picture or point-sighting hold before the identified target is fired upon.

Most people find that they can shoot better in the two-handed turret position in the dark, than they can, coordinating the pistol with the flashlight. The function of the flashlight is not so much to allow accurate shooting, as to allow one to spot and identify the opponent in the dark. By the time that is done, it would be foolish to drop the flashlight: instead, the shooter either fires at that point if it is warranted, or directs the beam of the flashlight into the opponent's eyes. It will depend on circumstances whether or not you fire at that point. Remember again that deadly force is only warranted to protect innocent life from immediate and otherwise unavoidable death or grave bodily harm, and that the man you are aiming the gun and flashlight at MUST possess the ability and immediate opportunity of doing so and be acting in such a manner that a reasonable and prudent man would assume he was using those powers to place innocent life in jeopardy.

Only when all those criteria have been fulfilled are you justified in exercising your nightshooting skills upon him.

Chapter 16

Handgun and Flashlight

An official of the National Rifle Association's police firearms training branch asked me once why Ray Chapman and I teach as many as five flashlight techniques to our students, in light of the fact that so few cops involved in actual gunfights use flashlights. I replied, "The statistics are like that because so few cops are trained to properly use their flashlights. If they were, more would be used in after dark shootouts, and there would be fewer tradgedies like the one in Staunton, California, where an officer without a flashlight fired at a shadowy, armed figure in the dimness . . . and killed a four year old boy holding a toy gun."

The function of the flashlight in a stress situation involving deadly weapons is manifold.

1. To find one's way to the situation, and back out again: in a word, illumination.

2. To identify the target positively before firing.

3. To blind the opponent as you fire, in that critical instant when you face each other across drawn guns.

4. To use as a self defense and arrest/control instrument if deadly force is not warranted.

5. To illuminate the target for better shooting.

Notice that lighting up the target so you can hit it better is the least of the reasons for coordinating the pistol with the flashlight. That coordination is, in most cases, so awkward that you will hit better in the dark, if there is any ambient light at all, by using both hands on the pistol and junking the torch. The flashlight is there for

FBI Flashlight Method: As discussed in the text, this technique has many short-comings on the street.

Flashlight Under Gun Method: This system works only with specially modified lanterns.

Photos Courtesy of *Combat Handguns Magazine*

118

tactical reasons, not reasons of marksmanship. The techniques presented here show you how to shoot well in *spite* of also holding a flashlight, not *because* you're also holding it.

FBI METHOD. The first of the flashlight firing techniques, and the poorest: the flashlight is held out and up, away from you, preferably also ahead. The theory was that the bad guy would shoot for the light. In fact, this does not work for several reasons.

Light from your flash can reflect off walls, showing you up while you sit there with false confidence thinking an opponent is going to fire at the flashlight. Punks know about this hold, and teach each other to shoot low and to the left of police flashlights. If you try to keep the light away from yourself, you unconsciously move it not only out but backward, thus unwittingly illuminating yourself, and if your gun is out ahead of you, it catches the flashlight beam and gives your real position away. The more you try to compensate for that by keeping the beam forward, the closer you bring it back to yourself, again unwittingly thinking that the beam is going to draw gunfire away from you.

The FBI position is very awkward to coordinate when firing a gun. It is best used for scanning an area while your body and most of your head are down behind cover. Even FBI stopped teaching it for shooting several years ago.

THE HARRIES TECHNIQUE. Developed by Mike Harries of the Southwest Pistol League, a pioneer in gunfight training, this technique was once state of the art. Several major academies still teach it as such. It has since been surpassed, however, by techniques that get arround its shortcomings.

In the Harries Method, the flashlight is held in a bludgeon position, with back of flash hand meeting back of gun hand. The two press together in an attempt to create dynamic tension that stabilizes the pistol. Depending on hand and flashlight shape, the light button may be controlled by little finger, index finger, or thumb. The idea is to flash the target and fire, change position, and do it again, leaving the light out while moving, of course.

The concept is valid and in application the method is vastly superior to the FBI technique. However, since back of hand mates with back of hand, recoil impulse tends to pull the gun away from the support hand. Also, the backs of the hand being convex, for most people the beam will go to the right of where the sights are or the sights will go to the left of where the beam is, creating the need for a last-second adjustment in a moment where there may not be an extra second left. The Harries technique requires a classic Weaver hand position to work well.

We are also concerned with safety hazards. It is very easy for the gun muzzle to cross the flashlight wrist when coming up into this

Harries Flashlight 1: Harries technique is designed to work w/flashlight in bludgeon position. Note that in stress draw situation, gun muzzle can cross wrist. Position is also fatiguing to hold for any length of time.

Harries Flashlight 2: Harries position in use. The first of the advanced pistol-flashlight techniques, still considered state of the art by many.

Harries Flashlight 3: This is the Farnam Improvement to the Harries technique: flashlight barrel is indexed on forearm. It makes beam and shot come closer together when shooting fast and somewhat reduces fatigue.

technique, and it is possible to smash the flashlight onto your gun wrist when executing the technique under extreme stress; indeed, with a long, multi-cell flashlight, you could conceivably "Kel-lite" yourself on the head. The position also does not work well when trying to bring gun and flashlight together while behind cover.

Another technique is to put the gun butt on top of the flashlight. This may work if you're holding a lantern, the top handle of which has been exactly custom shaped to fit the butt of your gun, but only this degree of customizing will carry out the technique's promise of the gun barrel lining up with the flashlight beam. With regular gun and flashlight, a round-butt revolver will shoot over the target, a 9mm. Smith & Wesson auto will shoot below it, and in any case, the gun bounces off the flashlight any time you fire it. A nice theory, but it doesn't work in the dark under stress.

The two flashlight techniques we emphasize at Lethal Force Institute are the Ayoob Method and the Chapman Method. The first is for close-range anti-personnel encounters, while the second is for intermediate distance situations and for searching.

In the Ayoob method, the key is "base of thumb meets base of thumb." At close range, when pointing at the chest, or even when aiming at eye level for most people, this angles the flashlight beam upward to automatically strike the suspect in the eyes as the gun is levelled at his chest. One starts with the flashlight in the conventional illumination position and the gun in conventional position in the strong hand; they come together with great speed. Since the gun recoils toward the open fingers of the gun hand, the other hand with the flashlight blocks recoil and increases recovery time much more effectively than the Harries position.

By the time you get back beyond seven yards, though, that upward angle of the flashlight starts to become too great, and the beam will go over the bad guy's head. For such intermediate distances, I've found the Chapman Method better. Ray developed it for winning night combat shoots — it's still unequalled for that — but it also has a place in night fighting with pistol or revolver.

To do a Chapman, you make an "OK" sign with your hand, encircling the flashlight with thumb and forefinger. The other three fingers go around the gun hand in an interlocking wraparound hold. For 9 out of 10 people, I find, it is most natural to work the light button with the thumb, as you would with the Ayoob technique. To align the barrel of the flashlight appropriately parallel with the barrel of the pistol, index the flashlight across the base of your thumb, at the "drumstick."

Now, your flashlight beam and your gunsights should be exactly in alignment. A good man with a good gun and a strong flashlight should be able to shoot effectively at up to 100 yards in total

Chapman Flashlight 1: Principle of Chapman Technique. Weak hand makes "OK" sign around flashlight leaving three fingers free.

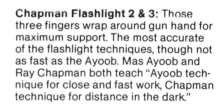

Chapman Flashlight 2 & 3: Those three fingers wrap around gun hand for maximum support. The most accurate of the flashlight techniques, though not as fast as the Ayoob. Mas Ayoob and Ray Chapman both teach "Ayoob technique for close and fast work, Chapman technique for distance in the dark."

Ayoob Flashlight 1: Principle of Ayoob Technique. Flashlight solidly held by one hand, gun solidly grabbed by the other, both meeting with "base of thumbs" as parallel felt index.

Ayoob Flashlight 2: When flashlight beam hits bad guy's eyes at close combat distance, the gun is ready to fire: just pull the trigger. If there is time to take a sight picture, powerful flash will give you ample illumination.

Ayoob Flashlight 3: Note that in Ayoob Technique, flashlight is automatically angled up directly into human antagonist's eyes within 7 yards.

darkness with this technique. It is slow to get into; that's why LFI students are taught that they should assume the Chapman hold if they are in searching mode with their flashlight, so it will be ready to go, and anything they flash their light on is already in the line of sights in a deadly danger situation. Obviously, that requires a great deal of fire discipline; I suggest a double action revolver. Seeing a person unexpectedly in the dark could cause your hand muscles to convulse, and I wouldn't want you to be holding a cocked handgun at that moment.

You will want the Ayoob Technique for speed situations in the dark at close range, and the Chapman Technique for when you have time to get your hands together right and are stalking in the dark, or shooting at distances. You will find that for any flashlight/ pistol technique, but particularly the Chapman, a slim C-cell light with no more than four battery cells will be much handier to operate, and such lights should be mandatory for people with small hands.

Chapter 17

StressFire Reload: Revolvers

As taught today in both police and private academies, the reloading of the double-action revolver is based on the "FBI Method". The right hand releases the cylinder and the left hand catches the weapon with the forefinger and middle finger going inside the frame and grasping the cylinder with the fingertips as the thumb actuates the ejector rod to punch the spent casings clear. This immediately frees the strong hand to go to the belt and be grabbing for fresh ammo while the empty brass is still being ejected.

It sounds great in theory. It *is* great in theory. It's pretty neat on the pistol range, too . . . but on the street, this method of reloading the revolver is extremely fumble-prone under stress.

When you dissect the conventional revolver reloading technique, you find a lot of things wrong with it that wouldn't have been apparent thirty to sixty years ago. For instance:

— In the conventional technique, the fingertips of the weak hand are holding the weapon. As we now know, the first area of the body to tremble violently during fight or flight reflex is the fingers of the weak hand. The lifeline to your survival of this prolonged gunfight is now held in those frail, trembling fingertips of your least dextrous hand!

— In the conventional technique, the tip of the thumb is used to actuate the ejector rod. The brass cases have been "fireformed" to the chamber walls inside the cylinder at 17,000 pounds pressure (.38 Special) to 35,000 pounds (.357 Magnum). If the gun is dirty, the brass is bad, or the chamber rough, that means they may not want to eject.

You have only a small amount of pressure that you can exert with the tip of your thumb . . . and that may not be enough to clear the cylinder and unjam the gun for reloading.

— When this FBI-style reload is done without intensive training and/or under pressure, there is a tendency for the gun to turn sideways, instead of being held with the muzzle straight up to allow gravity to help the spent casings drop out clear of the cylinder. This can mean spent casings sticking halfway out of the chambers (only one of which can block a whole speedloader full of fresh ammo), or even worse, can lead to an empty case being trapped under the ejector star, which renders the gun inoperable.

— When held in the conventional position, the gun barrel and cylinder are pointed somewhat sideways instead of perpendicular to the ground. This was all right back when FBI taught everyone to reload cartridges singly or in twos from the pocket, since the thumb could snap each cartridge firmly into place in its chamber. But today, we use "6 shots at once" speedloaders, and these depend on gravity in most models to seat the cartridges sufficiently for the cylinder to close the revolver mechanism to function properly and fire them.

With the gun held sideways, as happens automatically with the conventional FBI-style reload, a speedloader may not drop all 6 rounds into their chambers. If only one is still sticking out partway, the cylinder won't close and the gun can't fire.

— When executing the FBI-style revolver reload, the gun muzzle waves wildly in an arc that can even go over the shooter's shoulder. This is not in line with good firearms safety habits.

With all these things wrong with it, why is the FBI reload still so widely taught, even by relatively advanced private institutions? The answer is partly that rapid reloading techniques in competition have tended to concentrate around automatic pistols, and partly that conservative law enforcement was unwilling to let go of old training concepts that did not translate to such modern developments as speedloaders.

StressFire Revolver Speedload

In StressFire, we sought a technique that tied in with the fight or flight reflex, which makes the man stronger and faster, but clumsier, when facing a life or death battle. We wanted a technique that relied very little on fine motor coordination, but which would actually be enhanced by the gross physical strength that accompanies the adrenalin dump. Here's the technique:

When the last shot is fired, you open the cylinder just the way you would in the conventional method: the right thumb works the cylinder latch, and the tips of the left fingers push the cylinder out of the frame.

But in StressFire, *the gun handle stays in your right hand at this point*. Keep the thumb up, away from the back end of the cylinder, where it can also hold the cylinder fully out.

You tilt the muzzle straight up in the air, and the palm of your left hand comes down *once, sharply*, on the ejector rod. With the muzzle vertical and the ejector rod being hit hard, it is virtually assured that all spent casings will be punched clear and will drop straight down to the ground, out of the way. (See **StressFire Revolver Reload 1.**)

Now, the left hand comes in as in **StressFire Revolver Reload 2.**

StressFire Reload Revolver 1: Ayoob begins StressFire Reload of revolver, a technique adopted by virtually every department he has trained. Muzzle is vertical, thumb up and clear, and one sharp slap of left hand ejects even tight cases. Note hand is already off ejector rod; don't pump the rod, or case can get caught beneath ejector star.

StressFire Reload Revolver 2: Left hand comes in to grab gun. "V" between 1st and 2nd fingers encircles ejector rod ...

in a position best remembered by the gun buff as the exact same hand tracing you would send to Herrett's for a set of custom stocks. The three "lesser" fingers are together, the index finger is spread out as far as it goes in a "V", and the thumb is spread out in another "V".

The "V" between middle and forefinger encircles the ejector rod, and the thumb goes into the frame and locks the cylinder into its outward reloading position. *The gun is now held rock solid in a fist instead of in the finger tips, and the thumb is still free to turn the cylinder to more quickly accept cartridges fed in one at a time.*

The hand now lowers the revolver. You'll find that it is human instinct to "cup" a heavy object like the revolver, with the palm parallel to the ground. Held in FBI fashion, this would be holding the revolver's cylinder sideways and fighting gravity as the rounds were fed in . . . but in the StressFire technique, *the muzzle is perpendicular to the ground, and gravity feed is aided!*

Once the rounds have been singly chambered or the speed-loader has released its payload, grab the gun in firing position with the right hand, and close the cylinder firmly with the base of the left thumb. You'll find that the fingers almost magically "fall out of the way." Don't worry about casting the now-empty speedloader aside; just let go of it, and it will fall away as the cylinder is closed. Why waste a second throwing something aside when that something is going to be automatically dumped clear anyway?

As the left hand closes the cylinder (see photos) it is now in a perfect position to drop naturally back into a reinforcing Wrap-around or Ayoob Wedge hold on the weapon, instantaneously.

When you compare the standard technique to the Stressfire technique point by point, you find the following:

In standard revolver reloading, the tip of the weak thumb is relied on to eject casings, *but in StressFire's technique, a hard, firm, positive slap of the hand kicks the empties clear decisively.*

In standard revolver reloading, there is a tendency for the gun to be held sideways, reducing the likelihood of clear ejection of spent casings. *In StressFire, it is automatic and natural to hold the gun in such a way that the empties are punched clear.*

In standard revolver reloading, the gun is "instinctively" held (palm cupping weight) in such a manner that the gun lies sideways, making it difficult to reload with speedloaders. *In StressFire, the gun is automatically held in such a manner that the gun gravity-feeds smoothly from the speedloader.*

In standard revolver reloading, the gun is held in the feeble fingertips of the trembling, least dextrous hand. *In StressFire, the revolver is held in a solid fist.* If you doubt that, take your empty revolver in your weak hand in an FBI reloading hold, and see how

StressFire Reload Revolver 3: ... and thumb encircles cylinder as strong hand draws speedloader. NOTE FINGER POSITION ON LOADER: Fingertips are forward of bullet heads, so they can encircle the cylinder and "index" a perfect reload even in pitch darkness.

StressFire Reload Revolver 4: Insertion. Note how fingertips ahead of bullets guides the speedloader into place.

StressFire Reload Revolver 5: Knob is now released. This step can be skipped in one-stroke speedloaders like Safariland and Jetloader, but author prefers this HKS unit for durability and reliability.

StressFire Reload Revolver 6: Firing hand now takes position as weak hand closes cylinder. Note that speedloader is allowed to fall away by itself.

StressFire Reload Revolver 7: Virtually failsafe, the StressFire reload works even if you miss "V" finger placement around ejector rod. Here, all 4 fingers are around frame.

StressFire Reload Revolver 8: Seen from right, the rock-solid stability of StressFire reload is apparent. Note that muzzle is *naturally* perpendicular to ground, allowing smoothest working of gravity-operated speedloaders.

130

easily any assistant can rip it out of your hand. Now try it with the StressFire Reload hold: it is most unlikely that they can even budge it!

— In standard revolver reloading, the gun swings in an arc that can even encompass a range officer behind the shooter, not to mention the patrolman standing next to him on the firing line. *In StressFire Revolver Reload, the axis of the deadly gun muzzle never leaves the straight-on point of downrange toward the target!*

StressFire is safer to train with, but that is the least of its advantages.

The StressFire reload is MORE POSITIVE, MORE FUMBLE-PROOF, MORE FUNCTIONAL UNDER EXTREME STRESS than any other method yet devised for reloading the revolver under life-threatening pressure.

The StressFire reload is theoretically slower, if you go by "time and motion studies" with people who are under no stress. In practice, in the heat of competition, the author has used it to win state and regional championships, and an uncounted number of lesser competitions firing against accomplished men using the FBI technique. The secret, of course, was that competition delivers its own level of stress, and the fraction of a second difference between the two techniques was decided in the author's favor *because his technique worked better under pressure.*

Because it is easy to teach, natural and instinctive, compatible with speedloaders, and fumble resistant under pressure, the Stress-Fire Revolver Reload has been adopted by virtually every police department that ever sent one of their instructors to a Lethal Force Institute Course in Lethal Threat Management for Police, including the entire training program of the Idaho Peace Officers' Standards and Training Council.

Welcome to the Planet Earth, people . . . when professionals responsible for teaching police to deal with life-threatening criminal violence change their techniques, it's only because it has been proven to their experts that the new technique works better, under stress, for the man or woman caught up in that maelstrom of lethal savagery that can be dealt with only by the judicious use of deadly force, delivered by a man or woman only briefly trained in the best possible methods of coping with that threat.

Left-handed StressFire Revolver Reload.

Approximately one out of six officers are left-handed. They are forced to trust their lives to revolvers designed by right handed men, *for* right handed men. Here is how best to reload the revolver under stress if you are a southpaw:

StressFire Reload Revolver 9: StressFire reload technique for left-handed shooters.

StressFire Reload Revolver 10: Left thumb hits cylinder release latch as right thumb forces cylinder open. Thumb will follow through opening in frame as fingers encircle frame.

StressFire Reload Revolver 11: Because cylinder opens to the left, it is necessary for left hand to slap out empties. Muzzle is still vertical, slap is still sharp and clean.

StressFire Reload Revolver 12: Again, gun is held rock-solid and muzzle straight down as the more dextrous hand comes in with the speedloader.

132

StressFire Reload Revolver 13: Chambers loaded again, the thumb slides back out of frame, and supporting fingers are in natural position to close cylinder as left hand takes firing hold on grip.

Twist the gun in your hand as shown in the photo, with your left thumb hitting the cylinder release latch and the thumb of your right hand popping the cylinder out. Put your right hand in the same double "V" formation as a right-hander would do with his left paw, encircle the front of the frame, and smack that ejector rod sharply down with the palm of your left hand.

The gun is now held firmly by frame and cylinder with your weak right hand, as your more dextrous left hand goes for the speedloader. The cylinder is rotated, if necessary, with the tip of your middle finger, right hand.

As the speedloader dumps its payload, your left hand merely lets go of it and takes a firing hold on the gripframe. Your right hand now closes the cvlinder with its fingertips, and slides down into a support position to grasp the strong left hand and in a Wraparound or Ayoob Wedge position, as the speedloader falls away by itself.

Caution: you need a particularly sharp slap on the ejector rod when doing the StressFire Speedload left handed, since the positions of the fingers around the cylinder may partially block full travel of the ejector rod. In a right-handed reload, make sure at this point that the right thumb is clear of the rear of the cylinder.

Chapter 18

StressFire Reload: Automatics

For competition speed shooting with the autoloading pistol, it would be difficult to surpass the Gunsite Reload as developed and taught by Jeff Cooper. It works like this:

The gun is not run completely dry, but left "in battery" with a live round in the chamber and, ideally, at least one round in the magazine as well. When the decision is made to reload, the weak hand drops off the pistol and reaches for the spare at the same moment the strong thumb presses the magazine release button. A highly practiced man with good reflexes can learn to do it in a second.

The round is left in the chamber (a) to eliminate the need for the additional motion of thumbing the slide release as would be necessary when the slide locked back after shooting the gun completely empty, and because (b) in some types of pistols, this enables one to fire at least one shot if attacked while reloading. (The extra round in the magazine itself gives it more weight and allows a smoother drop from the butt).

On the range, this concept works superbly, but on the street, the theory has problems. Under the stress of real-life combat, once more than two or three rounds are fired, you're going to lose track of your "ammo count." Even such accomplished gunfighters as Jimmy Cirillo (5 reported kills) and Bill Allard (6 reported kills) told me that when it went beyond a couple of rounds, they fired until their revolver went click or their slide locked back. *In intense debriefings of over a hundred men who have been through armed encounters, I've not found ONE who was able to count his rounds accurately* after the third shot he fired!

Therefore, the person trusting an auto pistol for defense MUST be trained to AUTOMATICALLY operate the slide release if he runs his pistol empty! There is a concept that Smith & Wesson Academy has identified as "fire four, reload eight": the combatant with the automatic thinks he has fired only a few shots, then his gun won't fire, and when he looks down and sees the slide back, he initially believes his gun has jammed — but it turns out that he has fired all eight rounds.

I once polled the readers of AMERICAN HANDGUNNER magazine (130,000 circulation) and asked them for a single documented case where "the round saved in the chamber during reloading" had actually been used in a firefight. Not one was reported, nor have I ever run across such a case in real life. What *has* happened has been the hesitation of officers (in documented gunfights involving Illinois state troopers, for example) to *automatically* slam in the fresh magazine *and drop the slide* when the gun stopped firing.

I find that IPSC shooters attending my street combat courses, where I force them to run the gun dry, will fumble their reloads. The magazines are smoothly exchanged — and then the competitor brings his gun up and tries futilely to fire while his slide is locked back, because his previous experience has not trained him to slam the slide forward as an ingrained part of the reloading process.

Thus, the first principle in the StressFire Reload for Automatics is, *"Make it automatic to hit the slide release after swapping magazines."* If you have been fortunate enough to leave the slide closed, the movement of your thumb on the release catch takes virtually nothing away from your time, but may save you several precious seconds of fumbling in a "worst case scenario" gunfight.

Another phase of the competition reload that is dangerous when assimilated by someone training for the street is dropping the depleted magazine as soon as the weak hand lets go of the pistol. The day may come when you drop a magazine that still has a round or two in it, only to find out to your horror that when the free hand reaches the belt, there is no spare magazine there!

A great many lawfully armed citizens and off duty cops who wear automatics in street clothes do not bother to carry spare magazines with them, yet they have been trained on the range (while wearing a full range rig with at least one double magazine pouch) to execute a reload in the competition manner.

In 1979, outside Chicago, Trooper Ken Kaas of Illinois State Police district 15 was involved in a running gunfight just off the tollway. It ended up with Kenny barricaded in his squad car, exchanging shots with a punk who took cover behind his own vehicle with an automatic shotgun loaded with 20-guage slugs.

Ken couldn't remember if he had fired five shots, six, or seven. He considered reloading, but thought better of it because he felt his opponent was about to make a move. He was right: the man emerged from behind his vehicle and came at him, and Ken dropped him with what turned out to be the 7th shot in his 9mm. S&W model 39 automatic.

When he went to reload, he was shocked to find that the magazine was not on his belt. A short time before, at Inspection, a major had told him to remove the non-issue spare mag pouch from his duty belt. The magazine had been laying on the front seat instead, and had been lost inside the squad car in the violent bumping of the pursuit.

Had Ken done a competition reload, his spare hand would have found only empty air, the magazine with the round left in it might well have been lost, and the chambered round could not have been fired in that model pistol with the magazine out. Ken, with no other gun to reach, would have been helpless against the oncoming copkiller.

Thus, the second principle of the StressFire Reload for automatics is, *"Don't release the magazine in the gun until the reloading hand has already closed over the fresh magazine in the pouch."*

It is no great sacrifice in time to do it this way, and it can save your life. In 1982, Jon Winokur's excellent "Master Tips" column in AMERICAN HANDGUNNER magazine carried a series of illustrations showing how Mickey Fowler taught reloading an automatic. Fowler was a former national champion in IPSC and three time winner of the prestigious Bianchi Cup event of practical shooting — and in the illustrations, he waited to drop his depleted magazine until his reloading hand had already grasped the fresh one!

It is good to be quick, but it is *better* to be *positive*. A time and motion study would indeed favor the competition reload, but time and motion studies don't consider "human engineering" and human frailties — the "pucker factor," if you will.

The StressFire Reload, in which you are trained not to dump a partially full magazine until a completely full one is in your hand and in which you learn automatically to drop the slide forward if you have accidentally run your gun dry, covers you if you make one of the predictable, deadly errors that occur with a human being caught up in the cataclysmic violence of a gunfight.

Ask yourself which method makes more sense on the street.

The third principle is, *"If you've fired only a couple of shots, have the spare magazine and loaded pistol firmly in hand before attempting to execute a reload."* This is especially important if you haven't put in long hours making the reload from the belt pouch a pre-programmed maneuver that you can execute automatically.

StressFire Reload Automatic 1: LFI instructor Rick Devoid demonstrates Stress-Fire reload for automatic. NOTE THAT HE REACHES FOR SPARE MAGAZINE *BEFORE* EJECTING PARTIALLY DEPLETED ONE.

StressFire Reload Automatic 2: Once hand is securely on spare mag, Rick dumps the one from his .45. A southpaw, he uses left index finger instead of right thumb to hit release button.

138

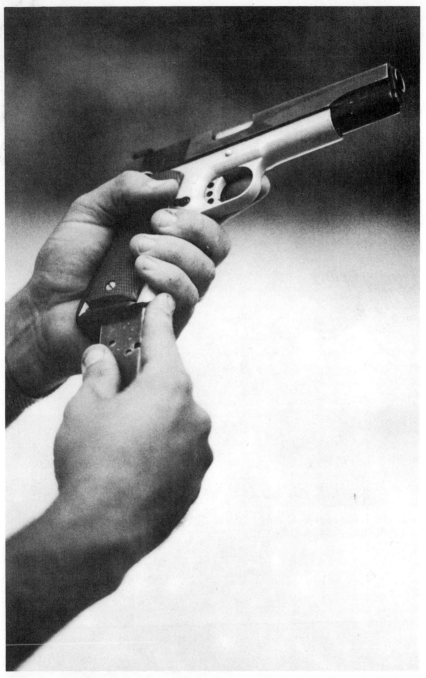

StressFire Reload Automatic 3: Rick inserts magazine (note that finger is off trigger).

StressFire Reload Automatic 4: Palm firmly slaps magazine home...

StressFire Reload Automatic 5: . . . and Rick is back firing in a StressFire Turret. In this sequence, there was already a round in the chamber, but Ayoob recommends half of all training be done with slide locked back.

Possibly the fastest reloading technique in IPSC simulated gunfighting competition is the technique first demonstrated by Tom Campbell of the US Team, and refined and first taught by world champion Ray Chapman. Generally known as the Campbell Method, it fits perfectly with the street concepts of StressFire, with one exception: Campbell does it by drawing pistol and spare magazine simultaneously, in competition, while on the street you would draw the magazine after the gun had already been drawn, and been fired at least a couple of times.

While behind cover during a momentary lull in the shootout, draw the magazine as shown in the photos. Most critical are the positions of the index finger and the little finger.

The index finger wraps around the magazine. The other three fingers go into a Wraparound position to support the firing hand. The little finger is completely clear below the floor plate of the magazine, a very important factor.

When you decide to make the mag change, hit the release button with your firing hand, and thrust the spare mag in immediately as soon as the depleted one has cleared. The little finger is the key, thrusting the magazine positively home. Now, depending on the immediacy of the threat, the dropped magazine may be either abandoned or retrieved. The hand is now ideally positioned to return to a wraparound or Wedge hold.

A variation of this is the "battlefield reload", taught for decades in Europe and first publicized in the US by combat master Chuck Taylor, a former protege of Jeff Cooper who truly came into his own as director of the American Small Arms Academy, as the "tactical reload." The principle was that, on a battlefield and cut off from supply depots, a soldier could ill afford to jettison even an empty magazine into the mud, let alone a partially depleted one, because there was no telling when he would be resupplied with fresh ones. It was cold comfort to win a skirmish in the morning with a fast reload, and be captured or killed in a second skirmish in the afternoon when the soldier ran out of magazines. Loose pistol ammo in bulk, to replenish empty "clips," is much more readily available to soldiers than spare handgun magazines.

This concept can be relevant to American street gunfighting as well. Picture yourself as a rural patrolman, cut off from his vehicle with his handy-talky smashed, shooting it out with an armed robbery team without hope of communicating a call for backup. Picture yourself as an executive forced off the road by two carloads of terrorist kidnappers, with only the 22 rounds in your loaded Colt .45 auto and its two spare magazines, to fight them off. You are as remote from "supply lines" as the loneliest soldier who ever fought for his country, and it behooves you to retain the few precious rounds in your partially depleted magazines.

First, *you want to be certain to make a "battlefield reload" while behind cover during a pause in the hostilities.* The magazine is drawn the same as in the standard "StressFire Reload" or "Gunsite Reload," in terms of positioning in the weak hand. The fingertip should be under the first exposed bullet, the thumb and two middle fingers alongside the body of the magazine, and the floorplate resting on the palm.

Put the heel of the hand under the pistol, and with the firing hand, eject the magazine, catching it with the heel of the weak hand. Take the ejected magazine between the third and fourth finger, and immediately slam the fresh magazine into the pistol, using the palm of the hand.

Now, the partially depleted mag may be put in a pocket, or re-inserted into the belt pouch. If you do the latter, *to keep the partially empty magazine from being confused with other full ones, insert it with the lip of the floor plate facing BACK.*

One of the things combat competition is good for is learning certain lessons less painfully than on the street, and that trick of backward-reinsertion of partially depleted magazines is an example. In 1979, in England, I competed in what was then the largest IPSC match in history, with nearly 800 international shooters, at Brisley's "Pistol '79."

Going into the final relay, or "flight" as it's called over there, I was running about third with a good chance of taking the whole thing with the last match, a speed event which was my specialty. I was helping out match director Nigel Hinton on one side of the range, when they called for the "last flight" on the one stage I hadn't shot yet.

Over I rushed, forgetting one thing: two partially depleted magazines from the previous flight were still in my belt pouch, uncharged. I loaded a full mag of Federal .45 ball into my Lawson Custom "Ayoob Special" Combat Commander, and took my position. I burned through the first three double-tap targets, did a competition reload, and my slide locked back after two shots. After recognizing the problem, I instinctively reloaded with the next magazine, which turned out to be full, but my score had slipped badly enough to drop me into 7th or 8th place overall. Since that time, every partially empty magazine I returned to my belt went in backwards, where my reaching hand could feel its position and instinctively reject it and go on to a properly placed, fully loaded mag.

While the revolver should be switched to the weak hand to allow the strong hand to perform the more dextrous task of reloading, the opposite is true of the combat auto. Shoving a big, fresh magazine into the pistol's butt requires comparatively little in the way of fine motor coordination, and much fumbling is saved if you keep the automatic in your strong hand and let your weak one carry up the fresh magazine.

Don't equip a street auto with an extended or oversized magazine release button! These tend to be accidentally released while the gun is in the belt or holster. Depending on whether or not your gun has a magazine disconnector safety (à la Browning P-35 and S&W 9mm.), you will then be unknowingly drawing either a one-shot pistol or a non-shootable weapon. One Northwestern officer was gravely injured when an overlength mag release button released in his holster, and his gun wouldn't fire at the close-range attacker who was chopping him up.

The right thumb (or left index finger for a southpaw shooter) should hit the release button while the weak hand brings up the spare magazine. The best carry and grasp of the spare magazine is that developed by Col. Jeff Cooper. The magazine goes into the pouch with the bullets and lip of the floorplate pointing forward. The hand comes down on it with the palm under the floorplate, knuckles forward. The tip of the index finger goes down along the front of the magazine, with the fingertip right under the topmost cartridge in the front.

At this point, the thumb and middle finger grasp the two sides of the magazine, drawing it upward, with the hand turning to a palm-up position. The index fingertip guides the magazine into the butt of the pistol (they don't call it the "index finger" for nothing!) and the palm of the hand now slaps the magazine firmly in place, as the already-opening fingers return to their Wraparound or Wedge position around the firing hand.

Smooth reloading is aided by two modifications: belling out the magazine well of the pistol at the bottom of the frame, and installing "base pads" on the floorplates of the spare magazines. The bevelled mag well tends to guide the magazine home, and the added length of the padded magazine makes a full insertion much easier and more positive.

Spare magazines should be padded, but not the one carried in the pistol, if it is to be concealed; the padded magazine lengthens the butt and makes it protrude more obviously under a jacket. That is also true of the Rogers E-Z Loader, a sort of bolt-on accessory that increases the effect of a bevelled magazine well. Excellent for competition, the E-Z Loader attachment will actually hamper your smooth reloading with a magazine that *doesn't* have a base pad.

Some teach the "battlefield" or "tactical" reload backwards, that is, taking the fresh mag betwen 3rd and 4th fingers and taking the depleted one in the strong fingers and palm. The fact is, the full mag is more important than the near empty one and should be held between the thumb and the first two digits, because the magazine held between the 3rd and 4th fingers is the one likely to be dropped under stress.

For reloading popular European-style pistols like the Heckler and Koch, SIG-Neuhausen, SIG-Sauer, or Browning BDA, one needs a different technique due to the butt-heel release catch that holds the magazine in place. The method I prefer is one I call "the hook."

As the weak hand comes off the pistol, the thumb and middle finger form a "C"-shaped hook. The thumb presses back the release catch, and the curved middle finger hooks the lip of the magazine's floorplate, ripping the magazine out of the gun.

The magazine is dropped and the hand continues with the momentum of the downward ripping-out motion, bringing it automatically to the spare magazine on the belt, which is then grasped and thrust into the gun butt as would be done with any other automatic. Thumb, forefinger, middle finger and palm, while executing "the hook," are in a perfect position for grasping the fresh mag and running it home.

Chapter 19

Your
Responsibility

If you've fully read this book by now you are thinking one of two things: either, "My God, I should put this book down before lightning strikes me, because this man is teaching total heresy in the known ways of pistolcraft!" or "Why the hell didn't I think of those things?"

If you're thinking the former, it's because you haven't tried the techniques yet. Never be so presumptious as to judge that which you have not seen and experienced. An open mind could have saved FBI training from being fossilized in the form it first was for nearly fifty years.

I was incapable of criticizing the FBI techniques until I learned them. I was a follower of the New Pistolcraft (sometimes called "the modern technique"), until I got deeply enough into the discipline to realize its shortcomings. Until the 1970's I, like so many other handgunners, ignored the martial arts because I thought my gun was such a uniquely American "Lazy Susan labor saving device for controlling violence" that I never bothered to look to the ancient arts that for centuries had refined the science of human coordination under great stress in the face of violence.

Fate gave me a unique opportunity to, for ten years, be paid to do what no man was ever so freely assigned before: to independently study gunfighting and police combat training to its greatest depth and breadth. The result of that experience was the formulation of the StressFire combat shooting system.

In the martial arts, Bruce Lee taught us to unleash our hands and eyes and subconscious from our aggressively intellectual human minds: to do what was natural for us when we were under pressure and had to fight to survive. His doctrine follows to the pistol. He taught us that the art must not form the man, but that the man must adapt the art to his own ability to function in the moment of truth.

Hundreds upon hundreds of students have been trained in StressFire to, in two days of shooting, equal or exceed the performance level they'd reach in a 40 to 56 hour police academy shooting program. That left the rest of their 40 hours free for me to teach them the advanced subtleties of tactics and mental awareness and preparedness, the only things more important to gunfight survival than combat shooting skill itself. The ease with which the students mastered StressFire, compared to one week courses where they had only fully grasped the Weaver and the New Pistolcraft techniques after all that time just shooting, proved the natural adaptability of StressFire to the human organism functioning under pressure with a gun it its hands.

This is not because StressFire is new and wonderful: it's because StressFire draws from the most proven techniques of both street combat shooting and the martial arts. Those who push the Weaver stance and the other New Pistolcraft theories point to this and that student who won a gunfight: NYPD can show over 800 rounds per year fired at criminals by their officers, with an 11-1 win/loss ratio. LAPD has an even higher ratio. Both use the bent knees, locked Isosceles hold, and eye level shooting techniques embodied in StressFire. Their street survival record far outweighs those of officers taught in the other techniques. Anyone who tells you, "Those people just don't know about our new pistolcraft techniques" is kidding you and himself; the combat masters of NYPD and LAPD long ago tested the "new pistolcraft" and discarded it as unworkable under stress without extensive training.

What StressFire did was to take the Turret and Isosceles holds in combination with the best of the New Pistolcraft, and go beyond it into traverses, one-handed techniques, and the best methods of champions like Ray Chapman to create, for the first time, a total system of fighting with the handgun under stress, within the parameters of the new knowledge of life threatening stress and its effects on the human body in terms of strength, coordination, balance and the other factors you've seen discussed.

The old style instructors of Police Combat Shooting have a copout. If their techniques fail they'll say, "I taught him marksmanship, but I couldn't give him courage."

They say every man has his own cop out. This is mine: "I showed you what you needed to know about shooting under stress when your life was at stake. If you were too obstinate, complacent, or lazy to try it and learn it, your death in a shootout falls on your head, not mine."

You have finished the book, and the ball is in your park now to study and practice the techniques shown. You must couple them with tactics and mental awareness.

Those two things are more important than shooting skill. You can be a state champion and die because a punk with a pot-metal .22 outflanked you and shot you in the back of the head. You can also die because even if you mastered combat shooting and tactics, you face a man who is prepared to shoot you when you haven't come to terms with your ability to shoot him yet . . . or worse, he outflanks you and shoots you before you even perceived yet that there was a danger to activate your already-honed readiness to fight skillfully.

My previous book, *In the Gravest Extreme: the Role of the Firearm in Personal Protection* — tells when to do it. *StressFire*, the first volume in a trilogy, tells how to do it. The middle volume will be titled *The Dark Place: Principles of Fear Control. Gunfighting for Police: Advanced Tactics and Techniques*, the final volume, will show how to get into position to do it, and ideally, to take that position so decisively that the opponent will surrender and you won't have to do it at all.

Understand that the use of deadly force against homicidal human beings is a complex and multidimensional discipline. It can never be learned from a book. It demands a commitment of mind, of spirit, of time — time in study, time in thought, time with a gun bucking in your fist in a manner that teaches you to control it under stress. It is a discipline that was taught too long by people who didn't fully understand its many and terrible ramifications.

If you wish to learn it you must study it to its depths. It will not be easy, but the knowledge you acquire will enable you to control the ultimate human violence at the personal level.

Good luck.

Keep your mind open.

Stay safe.

SUGGESTED READING

In The Gravest Extreme
by Massad F. Ayoob $9.95

Stressfire
by Massad F. Ayoob $9.95

The Semiautomatic Pistol in Police Service and Self-Defense
by Massad F. Ayoob $9.95

Fundamentals of Modern Police Impact Weapons
by Massad F. Ayoob
hardcover $15.95

Hit The White Part
by Massad F. Ayoob $9.95

Gunproof Your Children/Handgun Primer
by Massad F. Ayoob $4.95

The Truth About Self Protection
by Massad F. Ayoob $7.99

The Street Smart Gun Book
by John Farnam $11.95

Mastertips
by Jon Winokur $11.95

Police Handgun Manual
by Bill Clede $13.95

Police Shotgun Manual
by Bill Clede $13.95

Police Nonlethal Force Manual
by Bill Clede $15.95

Police Officer's Guide
by Bill Clede $19.95

Mostly Huntin'
by Bill Jordan $21.95

No Second Place Winner
by Bill Jordan $14.95

No Second Place Winner
by Bill Jordan
Spanish Edition $15.95

Bluesteel & Gunleather
by John Bianchi $12.00

Prices and availability subject to change without notice.

To order or to obtain a more updated version of our catalog, please write to
POLICE BOOKSHELF, P.O. BOX 122, CONCORD, N.H. 03302-0122 or call
our toll free 1-800-624-9049. In state, call 603-224-6814. We accept MasterCard
or Visa credit cards. Please add $2.95 to cover shipping and handling costs.